C000070021

# Fit-For-Purpose
# Leadership #4

## LeadershipGigs

WRITING MATTERS PUBLISHING

**Fit-For-Purpose Leadership #4**

First published in October 2018

Writing Matters Publishing (UK)
info@writingmatterspublishing.com
www.writingmatterspublishing.com

ISBN 978-1-912774-04-3 (e-book)
ISBN 978-1-912774-05-0 (pbk)

Editor: Andrew Priestley

Contributors:
*Health:* Suzie Volkes *Mindset:* Fanny Snaith, Michele Attias, Ali Stewart, Lorna Reeves, The Mo Bros - Kunal Dattani, Savan Dattani, Keval Dattani, Daniel Browne, Suparna Malhotra *Meaning and Purpose:* Dr Tina Allton, Alan Hester, Ryan Mathie, Dr Kylie Hutchings Mangion *Relationships:* Lesley Foley, Sandi Goddard *Best Practice:* Amanda Fisher, Mike Davis-Marks, Steven Shove, Andrew Priestley *Emerging Trends:* Natalie Jameson

Disclaimer: *Fit For Purpose Leadership #4* is intended as entertainment, information and education purposes only. This book does not constitute specific advice unique to your situation.

The views and opinions expressed in this book are those of the contributing authors and do not reflect those of the Publisher. The Editor, Contributing Authors, Publisher and Resellers accept no responsibility for loss, damage or injury to persons or their belongings as a direct or indirect result of reading this book.

All people mentioned in case studies have been used with permission; and have had names, genders, industries and personal details altered to protect client confidentiality and privacy. Any resemblance to persons living or dead is purely coincidental.

All contributing authors have signed a declaration that the submitted work is an original piece; and where required, all references include citations.

All images have been used with permission.

# Dedication

Dedicated to business leaders everywhere - and to you - someone who has decided to positively change *your* world.

# Contents

# About Leadership Gigs

*Leadership Gigs* was launched in 2017 as a global online community, for business leaders - CEOs, MDs, executives; SME business owners; and entrepreneurs. It was created in response to the need of business leaders for confidential, authentic, conversations with like-minded peers.

*Leadership Gigs* works because it allows leaders to connect on line with peers with a broad base of experience and from a diverse range of industries ... without the ads.

The glue, of course, is *Trust*.

Importantly, *Leadership Gigs* provides a confidential forum for sharing and discussing ideas, discussing, reflecting and receiving candid, constructive feedback. It allows members to share concerns, doubts, express vulnerability and get honest and direct support.

Feedback suggests that being able to talk freely with other business leaders reduces stress and isolation and leads to insights, key light bulb moments and breakthroughs.

# Welcome to Fit For Purpose Leadership 4

*Leadership Gigs* is a growing global think-tank of business leaders committed to sharing highly effective, best-practice.

In this book, contributors address six themes relevant to effective leadership:  *Health, Mindset, Meaning and Purpose, Social/Relationships, Best Practice* and *Emerging Trends.*

### What makes for a smart leader?

Recently, 100 senior business leaders were asked what they were looking for in an emerging leader. And who already had their attention; and why?

This is a broad summary of their responses. It is not intended as a checklist but it gives pause for thought.

The key traits include **qualified, smart, experienced** and **articulate.** And they must **have initiative** and be **relational.** But they must have **energy.** They must have spark.

A significant number mention **formal qualifications.** It was felt that a certain rigour underpins the attainment of qualifications, for example, obtaining a doctorate.

Many senior leaders admired smart people. By *smart* they meant people who exuded a cleverness, an intelligence and a confidence in their own thoughts and opinions.

Even if they said little they were recognised for insights, astute observations and even smartcuts - ideas with cut through.

There was something about the sharpness of thought.

A premium was placed on experience, track record and form. Theoretically, knowing what to do was valued but knowing exactly what to do under pressure was highly valued.

Most leaders polled complained about smart people who were incoherent. They wanted leaders who can be articulate, direct and concise. And clear.

Importantly, senior leaders are looking for initiative and this infers people who are both responsible and accountable. Right now we are experiencing unprecedented disruption and leaders want bright people who can pick a need or a gap, suggest a way forward and execute effectively. This doesn't have to be major initiatives. It might be something benign that enhances the qualitative experience of anyone connected to the business. But if you have ideas, don't sit on them.

Encouragingly, leaders are placing a premium on people who are relational. This doesn't mean sociable. It alludes to a deeper string of emotionally intelligent skills such as empathy and authenticity in communication. It acknowledges that the preferred work place cultures are preferred because meaningful collegiate and professional relationships are easy to create, build and sustain.

A recent UK poll of professional millennials reveals over 70% feel a CV does not allow an employer to know them as a person. And we know that disruption also brings with it staff attrition - notably, the trend of good people leaving bad bosses; and stagnant cultures.

Perhaps the most interesting; senior leaders are looking for energy. People who look and feel the business. When someone looks tired, bloated, sluggish and as if they are knocking on an empty tank it doesn't inspire confidence.

Importantly, if you are in a leadership role, what is shaping your leadership style? What resonates most from this short list?

What qualities do you value and how do you want to be seen?

With that in mind, *Fit For Purpose Leadership #4* explores some of the highest-value thinking around enhancing your personal and professional abilities as a leader in any sized business and any leadership context.

*Fit For Purpose Leadership* is organised under six categories:

- **Health:** Suzi Volkes explores issues directly related to your health and leadership.

- **Mindset:** Fanny Snaith, Michele Attias, Ali Stewart, Lorna Reeves, the Mo Bros - Kunal Dattani, Savan Dattani, Keval Dattani, Daniel Browne and Suparna Malhotra all provide their unique take on the mental game.

- **Meaning and Purpose:** Dr Tina Allton, Alan Hester, Ryan Mathie and Dr Kylie Hutchings Mangion explore meaning and purpose in a leadership role.

- **Relationships:** Lesley Foley and Sandi Goddard deliver two thought provoking articles on fostering professional relationships.

- **Best Practice:** Amanda Fisher, Mike Davis-Marks, Steven Shove and Andrew Priestley give four game changing perspectives on best practice and *'What does good look like?'*

- **Emerging Trends:** Natalie Jameson explores key directions in digital technology that is disrupting and driving business leadership.

Once again, business leaders, all at the top of their game, providing their highest-value thinking. Enjoy.

# Health

Physical health, fitness, exercise, wellness, wellbeing,
nutrition, diet, exercise, nutrition, sleep,
hydration, hormones, genetics, DNA

# Run Your Health Like A Business

## Suzie Volkes

As a leader you've worked hard to achieve your success and get to where you are. Constantly learning, adapting, improving. So much time and effort has got you to where you are now. You've poured hours into creating the successful business and career you now have. You've read the books, you've done the courses, you've worked with the mentors and coaches and learned from your peers to develop and fine tune your leadership skills.

Ask yourself why you've done this? Is it for you, for that feeling of success, for financial freedom, for early retirement, for your family, for more time to spend with your loved ones? In nine out of ten cases, what drives leaders to success is based on providing for their loved ones; and in the hope of having more time and financial freedom.

You might think about health and how you want to be healthy, feel good, look good and have more energy but finding the time is the difficult part. Leaders tend to be so focused on their careers and relationships, that health can be an afterthought or at least somewhere way down the list. Rarely if ever does it make the top two priorities. You might say it's third on the list of priorities, but is it really?

Leaders tend to find their time divided between their relationships and their work, and in many cases, the only time they can switch off is on holiday and even then after 48 hours they will be checking in to make sure everything is OK in their absence. You're probably in such a routine by now you rarely pay attention to what you eat unless it's in a new restaurant. You have your set exercises which you do when you have time and you have your set breakfast and lunch. Even when eating out you will opt for familiar favourites unless you have the luxury of time to sit, select and savour your meal.

We go through the motions on autopilot because our minds are focused elsewhere, we go to default and default isn't the same as what's best. Our brains like habits, they like familiarity, so if you always eat chocolate at 3pm Monday to Friday, you will crave chocolate at 3pm Monday to Friday. Just think, have you ever driven home and made it back without remembering the journey? Or a change in your routine means you've forgotten something?

Habits save mental energy for your brain so your brain likes habits whether they're good or bad.

That's why they can be so hard to break, as a familiar cue will trigger an automatic reaction which is in ingrained in you. You are where you are now because of your thoughts, your habits and your previous actions. If you are in the habit of smoking, you're a smoker or if you're in the habit of going to the gym then you'll be fairly fit.

Running on autopilot can have negative consequences on your health; weight gain, high blood pressure, high cholesterol, muscle wastage, low mood, low body confidence and low sex drive to name a few. Your career too can suffer; your concentration becomes poor, your energy drops, you lose motivation, you become grumpy and stressed and start to hate the job you once loved.

You'll say you just fell out of love with it but is it the work or is it your health? As your productivity drops, you'll find it harder to get the work done in the hours you have. You'll resent the fresh talent who comes through the door and start counting the days until your holiday or even retirement. All from letting your health run on autopilot.

Would you let your business run on autopilot? Sure the idea of passive income is a great one, but how would that help you grow, improve and develop? If it all ran on autopilot, the world would move on and you'd be left doing the same things over and over.

How many once successful businesses didn't change, adapt and improve and where are they now?

## Running your health like a business.

As leaders, you've achieved your position through putting time and effort into your career so why would you not do the same with your health? Is your health worth investing in?

Being healthy gives you more time through improved concentration and you're more productive and have the drive to grow and develop your business.

This, in turn, gives you more time to spend with loved ones and enjoy it more too with elevated mood.

Being healthy gives you more money because of the direct impact it can have on your career and business.

Being healthy means you enjoy life more because you have more energy, better mood from the endorphins and reduced aches and pains meaning you want to get out and enjoy life more.

If you're not running your health like a business, your body could be about to go bankrupt.

So how can you run your health like a business?

## Planning

Starting a business, growing your business, there's always a plan. How to get from A to B. We massively fail to do this with our health. Instead, we set loose intentions for a goal a few months away that are difficult to achieve as the old habits creep back in.

Is that how you write a business plan? No, you do the research, you analyse the obstacles, you work out the financial forecast, work out what you'll need and set short, medium and long term goals. You would put so much effort into a business plan to ensure success so think what would happen if you put effort into your health.

Could you run your business by working on just a three month half wishful goal? Would you think you kind of know what you're doing so you'll just give it a go? You wouldn't run your business like this, so why do it with your health? Play the long term game; set one year, three year and five year goals. Do your research, plan for obstacles, figure it out, make sure it's realistic and know what you need to do to achieve it.

## Project managing

Within the plan there will be projects. It might be to improve your diet through eating more fruit and vegetables, or to be able to do 50 push-ups or to achieve eight hours of undisturbed sleep every night. Whatever your goals within you health business plan, your projects need some individual attention.

1.  Get specific. Know what you want to achieve and when by and make sure it complements your five year vision.

2.  Identify your project team. Who can support you? Do do you need assistance from?

3.  Identify the steps. Break it down, do the research to understand the steps required to achieve the project goal.

4.  Define clear milestones for example you want to increase

how much water, set milestones for the amount you to drink daily and plan the increments over a few weeks and months.

5. Stay open and honest about progress. Frankness and tracking is key to ensuring progress is being made.

6. Manage risks. What are your biggest obstacles and how can you stop them having a negative impact on your life?

7. Test progress and evaluate. Is it working? If not, why not? Makes changes.

You wouldn't decide to run a marathon today and run it tomorrow, no, you'd follow a plan and build on it step by step. You might set a goal of a 5km run and work towards that, then a 10km, then a half marathon and then a marathon. You know you can achieve the bigger goal if you follow the plan for your mini projects, so it's the same here. Set your long term strategy and implement your project management skills.

## Bringing in experts and recruiting a team

Whether it's for a project or for a long term strategy, getting help from experts in their field can make a significant impact on the overall quality of the outcome and the speed in which this can be achieved. Think about who is specialist that can help you with the area you need to develop. Is it a trainer to help with the exercise, is it a dietitian for nutrition, is it a physiotherapist for recovery or pain, or is it a counsellor or NLP practitioner to help you with your mindset?

Sure you can do it yourself just like you can with anything, but the question is: is it worth spending a lot more time and effort for possibly a less effective outcome just to save some money? If it was your business would you compromise on results for saving some money or would you bring a specialist in to help you? Just like anything, the word cheap and best do not go hand in hand.

Figure out which expert you need and invest like your life depends on it, because it does.

Whilst the experts in their field can help with a specific outcome, you'll find you'll also need a team. If you've ever been in a role where it's just you or you've grown a business from being a solo entrepreneur to a thriving business you'll know how difficult it can be to go it alone.

If you have no one to bounce ideas off, sound off to or support you, things can get a little testing and doubts creep in.

When you're crushing old health and fitness habits and forming new, willpower alone won't see you through.

Willpower and motivation will get you started but it's the habits that will keep you going so until those new habits are firmly ingrained, you need a support team.

Much like in business, you have your highs and then there are days that you think, why do I do this? There's a reason weight loss groups work so well and peer support plays a huge role in that. Now you don't have to join a group but certainly find your friends, colleagues or family who are health focused and surround yourself with these people. Also try and get your friends and family involved as much as possible in new healthy habits, you'll find the journey easier and more enjoyable by having a team around you.

## About Suzie Volkes

Suzie Jane Volkes is the director of *Be Valkyrie*, a personal trainer and health coach. Suzie is a champion bodybuilder which was achieved whilst working in a corporate role and travelling around the World. Suzie's specialist competitor knowledge and background in healthcare helped shape and develop *The Valkyrie Solution*, her unique methodology, which has been designed with the busy professional woman in mind.

*Be Valkyrie* specialises in health and weight loss for female executives. The unique methodology *The Valkyrie Solution*, focuses on helping women transform their health, bodies and lifestyles from a place of struggle around feeling time poor, confusion around what's right for them and a lack of confidence in themselves and their bodies to one of improved health, strength and confidence.

Suzie has experienced and seen others experience personal, physical and mental transformation through the mode of health and wellbeing. The mission is to improve the lives of women by breaking down obstacles and limiting behaviour so they can reap the benefits in their personal lives and career from leading a healthy lifestyle.

www.thevalkyriesolution.com

info@thevalkyriesolution.com

Facebook: @bevalkyrie

Instagram: @beavlkyrie

Twitter: @bevalkyrie

LinkedIn: Suzie Jane Volkes

## Mindset

Psychology, motivation, development, experience, upbringing, self-talk, emotions, feelings, resilience, emotional intelligence, self-worth, perceived ability to control, mental health

# If Money Was Your Lover

## Fanny Snaith

It is assumed that if we earn a shed load of money we will be financially successful and to be financially successful we need to earn a shed load of money. As a Money Coach I know that is just not so.

Many high earners end up skint or bankrupt – we read it in the papers all the time. *"Premier League Footballer goes bust"*, *"£5m lottery winner back on the dole"*. Rags to riches stories, amazing tales of financial tenacity are abundant too.

I am not going to describe in detail how people spend way beyond their means, pay high interest on credit cards, have finance deals on snazzy cars, gigantic mortgages that they cannot afford, or even labour the point of how people shut down all sense when it comes to planning and saving for the future. I will, however, focus on how to become financially successful without totally relying on the monthly pay packet. I will encourage you to take action now, as time is of the essence when it comes to growing money and achieving long term wealth, and it is never too late to start.

Follow these three steps and you will be on the road to financial freedom.

## Number One – If money was your lover

One of the first questions I ask my clients is, *"If money was your lover, how would you describe your relationship with it? Would it be warm and close? Do you just about tolerate each other? Or, are you currently living apart?"* While the responses vary, they generally tell me that it would be a relationship they consider far from ideal.

Many of us live with fear, greed, anxiety, and shame around money, but we make little attempt to understand why we have these feelings or where they came from.

Compounding this, it seems we don't like to talk about these feelings. We feel that we are alone – but I can assure you we are not. Keeping repressed negative feelings about money silent, keeps us trapped and unable to make better choices to create the lives we dream of.

Our relationship with money is shaped by our *money story*.

From early childhood, money plays a huge part in our lives. As children we hope and dream of having plenty of money. We fear not having enough money. Money often defines who we are. We make life decisions based on money. Developing an emotional connection with money is inevitable.

Our first experience with money is where the story begins. Our stories are all different – some dramatic that take twists and turns like an adventure movie, some are stories of shame and embarrassment which people prefer not to share.

We rely on parents, grandparents, siblings and teachers to be our role models. Like a sponge, we absorb what they do and say. We look to their knowledge to teach us how to be. But what are we taught? What do we see? And how does this affect our relationship with money in later life?

It is critical that you understand your story – be able to see it objectively and consciously.

To do that start by asking yourself:

- What is my earliest memory of money?
- What was the experience like?
- How did that experience affect me?

Ask these questions for as many money experiences and observations that you can recall. Think of the key people in your story and how significant they were.

What messages, patterns or behaviours related to money did you learn from them?

I suggest you write your money story down. Order it chronologically. You can then read it back taking a helicopter view and gain new perspective.

When you have completed your money story, ask yourself these questions.

- How does my personal story affect my relationship with money now?
- What beliefs, values or judgments about money are related to my personal experience and family history? Are they still active today?
- Are they working to serve me, or not?
- Am I having the kind of relationship I want to have with money, or not? How could it be better?

Understanding your behaviour around money is key if you want financial success. As a money coach, I see clients who are keen to achieve financial freedom, but just can't seem to *make it.*

Stories unfold of plans to reach financial freedom, only to find them failing as limiting beliefs, excuses or diversion overrides intention.

Every person I have worked with, who chooses to discover and understand their true relationship with money, has been able to find a better and easier way to hop onto and follow the path to financial freedom. Indeed, if we are to live a balanced healthy life in both mind, body and spirit then a harmonious relationship with money is near, if not top, of the list.

## Number Two – Money In, Money Out

Watching the money coming in but not paying attention to the money going out will only take you to one place - financial misery. Nobody can survive financially with a *leaky bucket* – but knowing that it is leaky in the first place is key – and *where* it is leaking, too.

It matters not one jot whether you earn ten thousand or a million pounds. Get present and start managing your money like a part-time business. Nobody cares about your money as much as you should do – and that includes your accountant, your bookkeeper or your financial advisor.

As a leader in the workplace, you will have managed teams of people and budgets. Personal finance is exactly the same. Be conscious of your money flow by allocating time and patience to it.

Get the numbers to work! If the monthly payment on the lease car is too high, or the mortgage is strangling you – change it! By the way the word mortgage comes from the French meaning death-pledge. French peasants worked until they died for the privilege of owning a house! Sound familiar?

If you haven't already, start investing and look for passive income streams – these are ways to earn money while you sleep. Search passive income streams and beginners guide to investing on the web to find all you need to get you started.

Discover a way of running your personal budget that works for you. It may be an app, a spreadsheet, envelopes with cash or a piece of paper – anything that you will use consistently. Track your spending. Stick to your budget. I use my own system of *Money Mapping*, which helps me spread annual fees across the year and save for holidays and Christmas. This smooths cash flow – just the same as you would expect your accounts person to do at work. Your money is important, it is your new part-time business – RUN IT WELL!

### Number Three – Set Goals!

Now that you are better acquainted with your money mindset and know how your money flows, set goals – BIG GOALS.

Goals provide a place for focus, a sense of achievement – knowing where you want to go and then finding the tools and guidance to get there. Do, however, remain flexible with your goals. Rigid goals in an ever-changing financial climate will not serve you – allow change but avoid diversion.

Ask yourself *where* you would like to be financially.

Also ask *why*. Essentially, this qualifies your goal. Qualification is necessary as purpose is vital. A rudderless goal serves no one. Setting goals will determine how much you need to make, save and invest. It quantifies your ambitions.

I love this quote by Alexa Von Tobel:

> *"A good financial plan is a road map that shows us exactly how the choices we make today will affect our future."*

So, there you have it. Realise that money is so much more than numbers. We make so many decisions based on our emotions around money – where we live, shop, what we drive etc. Money is the best tool to give you choices in life. Look after it.

We don't need to have the best phone or the best car just because everyone else has it. You have no idea if they actually own it or if it is on tick! Be cool – don't just *look* cool.

To be financially successful you don't need to earn a shed load of money, you just need to treat it like a devoted lover.

Be your own person, know your own money flow and manage it like a part-time business. It is so much easier being you than pretending to be someone else – if you need help with that, find yourself a Money Coach to help you. We all need coaches – in all areas of life, including money.

Personally, I will be financially free. It won't take long now. I have been working on it for a good few years. I am excited for when that day comes. I don't live in the biggest house or drive an expensive car – I don't really look cool, but I am pretty cool money wise.

If money was my lover, we would be having a great relationship – very warm and close! What about you?

## About Fanny Snaith Certified Money Coach(CMC)®

Fanny Snaith lives in Cheltenham, in the UK. She is not an accountant or an IFA. In fact, she has never worked in financial services. She has, however, had plenty of experience with people and money.

Having watched her mother lose a large inheritance though careless spending and poor money management, Fanny made the vow to tread a different path. She trained and worked as theatrical stage manager, worked in the television industry as a production manager and spent thirteen years as a credit controller for a consultancy firm with bases in the US and the UK.

Now working as a Certified Money Coach(CMC)® and Couples Money Coach she enjoys working with people to understand and change their relationship with money so that they can experience their greatest financial and personal potential.

Fanny is committed to helping the world better understand the meaning and purpose of money in our lives. She believes that talking about money, discovering and challenging our belief systems about money, can only make us and the world engage better with the wonderful tool and resource money is meant to be.

www.fannysnaith.com

www.linkedin.com/in/fannysnaith

https://twitter.com/FannySnaith1

# Leadership Mindset

## Michele Attias

As I reluctantly started my first day working at a mental health organization over 30 years ago, the manager in charge of the new recruits, posed a powerful question to me.

He asked, "Where are you coming from?"

As I looked on surprised and confused, he continued.

"Because once I know where you're coming from, I know where you're going."

As a slightly hesitant woman in her twenties, about to navigate her first professional role, I didn't quite understand the question, or his subsequent answer. But as life has afforded me so many opportunities to understand this powerful, yet simple question, I now understand that it all starts within.

Where you come from is everything.

It all starts with your internalized mindset, which affects your motivation, purpose and intention, which determines the direction you move towards and all that sprouts forth.

Leadership is more than a title, status or role.

It is an embodiment of qualities creating a ripple effect which manifested outwards, create an external impact. It allows those who relate to you to react based on your inner leadership stance.

This is not just confined to the walls of an office, but you carry it wherever you go, like that companion who walks alongside you determining each action you take.

We are all born into a system called life.

Within this system, we incorporate our family, culture, religion and community. Finding our place in life and then having to take on the responsibility of leading others requires a certain penchance and capability.

It's not for the faint hearted.

We all knew kids at school who were natural leaders, they hadn't completed a leadership training or attended any workshops, yet wherever they stood in the playground broodily looking on, other children would surround them like bees to a honeypot.

They exuded an inner confidence and self-belief that was innate, and others followed. This playground leader could wear the most mismatched outfits, the most hideous haircut, but all his *followers* would follow on obligingly.

The effortless stance of being completely at ease with who they are, and letting go of being a leader, had the effect of becoming even more effective as one. No effort or energy being spent forcing or cajoling others to follow.

It is somewhat like the Rolls Royce. This car commands respect. It doesn't need to rev its engine any louder than other cars. It does not come in bright colors to attract attention, instead it is simple, silent, understated, but carries a hugely powerful presence. The internal engine of the Rolls Royce is pristine, robust and shouts quality.

I coached a client recently who was struggling in his leadership capabilities. He had never been respected in any of his roles as a manager, and had tried hard to be liked, taking constant actions within his company so he could to gain recognition, acknowledgment and praise.

To his chagrin, he was generally ignored, dismissed and demeaned. But he had missed one very important point.

Leadership is not about *what* you're doing, it's about *who* you're being.

So what is your inner stance? By this I mean, where do you come from?

There are various mindsets that can potentially impact your state, and it's important to recognize when you're operating from one of them. Do you lead from a soulful place of compassion, love, empowerment, or from a state of anxiety, insecurity, stress and anger?

This requires you to be aware of the mindset that is driving your behavior.

Remember that we live in a thought created reality and your thinking creates your feelings, which then creates your experience in the moment. Feelings are not created in a vacuum, they are always powered by thought, and as approximately 60,000 thoughts a day and 48 thoughts a minute enter your mind, the process can become a high voltage scenario which can get in the way of gaining any measure of clarity.

This isn't about changing your thoughts into positive ones, or becoming the thought police as a feeble attempt to stop your thinking.

It's about knowing that we don't need to take some of these thoughts seriously, or attach, internalize and personalize them. They are thoughts often powered by the ego, carrying decade's worth of insecurities, regrets and juvenile dialogue.

The thoughts driving you could be *'I'm not being respected,' 'I'm going to fail,' 'I have to be perfect,' 'I have to know it all,' 'No one ever listens to me,' 'It's not going to work.'*

Imagine attempting to step into leadership with any selection of those thoughts running through your mind.

Ask yourself: which thoughts are getting in the way of your leadership?

Imagine if those thoughts were no longer there, how would you lead differently? What benefits would this have on your team?

I teach my coaching clients to step up into leadership from the offset. Which means they need to take responsibility for their growth during our work together. As they approach their first coaching session, I observe as my clients look to me for guidance, as a child looks onto a parent. It's as if they have handed the baton of the responsibility of their growth to me.

At times, I have had to step up my own leadership stance substantially, and this is important, as clients will often attempt to push the boundaries on all levels, whilst I need to stand firm. Allowing the boundaries to be pushed simply does not serve the client or our work together. My role is to model this for them, and this can present with challenges.

As an example of this; I was coaching a highly successful businesswomen who was extremely disorganized and vacant. She consistently turned up late for her sessions and seemed to lack the commitment needed to succeed in coaching. This experience was making me feel angry, disempowered and disrespected, therefore making this exchange more about my ego being tarnished.

I discussed this case with my own coach who picked up the anger in my voice.

He swept my ego to one side for a moment and asked me: "What would best serve your client?"

I sat in silence for a while as I realized how enmeshed I had become in my clients process.

We all have buttons which when pressed; resemble a *Jack in the Box* toy. Once you push a particular selection of buttons, the *Jack in the Box* pops up. That is how your ego pops up when it feels threatened. Those buttons belong to decades of situations and scenarios that are highly charged with sensitive content.

I reflected on my client with compassion, I recalled that the reason she had wanted coaching was because she felt disrespected by her own clients and although she had limitless potential, she was struggling with being taken seriously as a professional.

Despite the fact that she had already paid me for a three month coaching programme which was non-refundable, I stepped up into leadership from an inner state of compassion and a focus on doing what would best serve her, whilst being unwavering in what I was willing to tolerate from this client.

I drafted an e-mail to her, and in my communication, I told her that I had chosen not to continue to coach her at the present time. I did not want to invest more on what she wanted than she was prepared to. Once she was ready and prepared to show up for the sessions and engage in them fully, she could resume the sessions. However long this took for her to be ready, however for the moment, I would not schedule a further session until she could commit to keeping to our agreements.

She did not respond to my communication immediately.

Six months later, I received a short e-mail from this client where she stated sheepishly "Michele, I'm ready to re-start our sessions."

I can't stress how different this client was once we re-started our work together. She was engaged, present, focused and not only did she complete the sessions, but she happily referred other clients to me.

Had my leadership included confronting her angrily, because I was feeling disrespected, it would not have had the same result.

In discovering the mindset that was leading my state, I was

able to turn it around; focus on leading not from anger, but from what best would serve my client in her growth, whilst honoring myself in the process.

This changed the dynamic, the communication and all that happened after.

At times we are too caught up in our own processes to be fully present with what is unfolding around us. It's important to slow down, become aware of the buttons that are being pressed, and reflect on what your inner motivation is. In this way, those who you lead are drawn to you because you embody a presence, which appreciates, acknowledges, collaborates with and motivates others.

A leadership presence which does away with hierarchy radiates authenticity and inspires those around you.

## About Michele Attias

Michele Attias originates from Gibraltar and currently lives in London. She is a Mindset Expert, Executive Coach, International Speaker and Author of *Look Inside: Stop Seeking Start Living.* She was previously a registered and accredited Therapist.

Michele coaches professionals to optimize their mindset and become better decision makers and action takers without the over-thinking, stress, anxiety or burnout. Her unique methodology combines the most powerful aspects of Coaching, Deep Mindset work and life Design drawn from spending over 15 years working in the psychological field.

In 2014 she was a finalist in *The Women Inspiring Women Awards*, and in 2017 was a *Best Coach* finalist at the *Business Women Awards* in the UK. She has also been featured in Gibraltar TV, Media and speaks internationally at events and conferences.

She's a passionate writer for online platforms such as *Thrive Global, Lifehack, Medium, LinkedIn, The Start Up, Inbound, Personal Growth* and *Vunela.* She shares her inspiring articles on optimizing the mindset with over 30,000 subscribers on these platforms.

Her philosophy when coaching, writing or public speaking is based on a basic principle: Outer world success should not come at an Inner world price.

Website: www.micheleattiascoaching.com

Linkedin: https://www.linkedin.com/in/micheleattiascoaching/

# A Critical Mindset for Leaders

## Ali Stewart

As the accrediting body for an award-winning leadership programme, I was running a masterclass for a group of my *Liberating Leadership* practitioners recently and I asked them questions like:

- What one model do you wish you had known about when you first became a leader of people?

- What one model makes the biggest impact on performance when you share it with your clients?

- Looking round the room what jumps out at you as the single most helpful thing leaders need to know?

It didn't matter how many times I asked the question, or in how many different ways I framed it, the answer was always the same. They said it was the mindset of truly *Liberated Leaders*.

The problem we find is, if you operate some of the leadership models you learn in isolation from the mindset, they tend not to work nearly as well. We teach a four-step leadership process, however, this process won't work unless we start with the underpinning mindset. If we don't have the right mindset we can come across as glib and not really caring, it's difficult to get people to follow us or carry out tasks the way we would like them done. And, of course, the mark of a great leader is one who has followers.

## A mindset with depth

This mindset has been well researched and documented by a number of different sources, it even stands alone as a model you have probably come across before. But until you connect it with the underpinning principles of high performance leadership, you won't appreciate its fundamental importance.

We are talking about the mindset of *High Challenge* and *High Support*, used in powerful and equal combination. This is the absolute sweet spot for leaders. However, what we find with all the thousands of leaders we have profiled, is that most are skewed towards one or the other. See what it's like for you.

Do you:

- A. Push people like you do yourself, and get frustrated when they can't work as quickly as you?

Or do the exact opposite, and

- B. Try to be everyone's friend and end up doing all the work yourself?

You will see that A is more *Challenging*; B is more *Supporting*. The need to have them in combination is paramount.

Imagine what happens in an organisation where there is a very high level of *Support*, but not much *Challenge*. When we ask a group of leaders this they usually say, it might be quite nice, you wouldn't have to work too hard, it could be relaxed and happy, or it could be a bit tedious. What you get is mediocre performance, no-one is ever challenged to be the best they can be. Often the manager is doing the work, finishing things off for people, correcting mistakes, not wanting to add pressure if they think the team member is busy.

And the opposite tends to happen where you have *High Challenge* and a low level of *Support*.

Groups report that in such situations there is high stress, people would be constantly watching their backs, fearful of putting a foot wrong. It is demotivating. Some may rise to the challenge, but high performance is at best random, and staff turnover is high. Often the manager is pushing staff because of limited resources and time. The task is supremely important and, in their mind, only the best will succeed.

*Low Support* with *Low Challenge* - have you ever been in a situation like this? What is your experience? Some quite enjoy the fact that no-one is on their back, pushing them to get their work done, but most fall into a level of apathy, because no-one is paying them any attention at all. Typically, you get poor performance, people are so unmotivated to achieve, because nothing ever happens anyway. Often the manager is feeling disenfranchised, doesn't know which way to turn, struggling themselves to know what to do. This sometimes happens in times of great change.

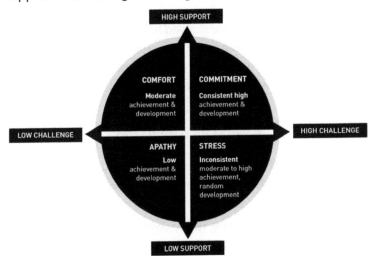

And the opposite of course is where we have both in perfect combination. Both *High Challenge* and *High Support*. Maybe that's the kind of environment you are in right now? When asked during training sessions, leaders usually say there is trust, excitement, team working, commitment, enthusiasm, a willingness to push boundaries and achieve, people feel listened to, people feel as if they matter. This is where consistent high achievement and development occurs, this is where the leader has set the vision for the team, and everyone knows what to do. This is when teams become noticeably high performing and others are keen to join the team.

## It works for business leaders

I'm currently working with the owner of a highly successful business. He thought he was leading through his people by providing a wonderful environment for them: lovely offices, the latest equipment, great kitchen, lovely relaxed meeting-eating area. Although providing the right environment is important, when we started work on the mindset of *High Challenge-High Support,* he realised for the first time he had been doing all this because it made him feel good. When we tested him, his scores showed he was more skewed towards *Support.* Now he is going to share his vision, set the ground rules, and start operating with a better balance of *High Challenge-High Support,* and take his people from good to sensational.

## It works for parents too

I first felt the full weight of what it meant to operate with *High Challenge-High Support,* when our son Sam was about 15 years old and very unruly.

Just to back track slightly, the reason I know about all this is because I've written two books on it, and have worked with Dr Derek Biddle, chartered occupational psychologist for over 25 years. We built a management consultancy, and together tried and tested what is now the *Liberating Leadership* programme with all of our clients over many years.

At over 80 years old, Derek has long since retired, but he is still my guide and mentor.

In the programme there is a brilliant *Performance Navigator,* which helps leaders to get to the nub of performance issues. As you work through the *Navigator,* taking all the remedial action suggested, you may reach the bottom box – which says *redeploy.* By that stage you appreciate the person has neither the skill or will to do the job.

Coming back to Sam, he was growing, finding his way, thought he knew it all, didn't hold back from answering back in class, or punishing his classmates for their wrong-doings to him – which got him into trouble. His behaviour was so bad, we were called to school weekly to discuss things. I thought I had tried doing everything I could to help the situation. Then when Sam was excluded for a couple of days, I remember calling Derek in despair, complaining that I couldn't redeploy my children!

He said quietly, "Ali, go back to the beginning."

The beginning is *High Challenge-High Support* and all the principles which underpin that fundamental mindset. The full weight of realisation hit me. Because of my personality type, I generally see the good in people, make excuses for their behaviour, keep the peace, smooth things over, help unite warring parties. I had been far too supporting. So, I went about upping the *Challenge.* It was hard, it meant withdrawing my attention when it was not deserved. It meant laying down some rules and following through consistently.

There was even an occasion when Sam did something so bad, that my husband and I decided the punishment was that Sam could not go on the planned ski trip with the school. As a mother, it broke my heart that he couldn't go, that he was denied this amazing opportunity, but as a leader I knew he absolutely could not go.

When I share this story with other parents they admit they would have succumbed and let him go.

But Sam knew that it was a fair punishment for what he'd done. If we had let him go he would have lost all respect for us and would have become completely unruly.

Sam is now the most amazing young man with tremendous self-leadership. He has been working since the age of 16 and now at 24 has a great job, is getting married and buying a house.

It takes resilience to be a *Liberated Leader*. You need to keep yourself in a strong, grounded state to be of the best service to your people and yourself. There are many articles in this book and previous books in the *Fit-for-Purpose* series to help you.

And having *High Challenge* and *High Support* in perfect balance is key. If you need help working out how to do this, you'll find more resources on my website. Or do get in touch, I would love to chat with you.

## About Ali Stewart

Ali is an award-winning leadership coach, mentor and best-selling author. She specialises in coaching fiery, dynamic leaders, in danger of burning themselves out.

She has built two successful businesses in training and development. She founded *Ali Stewart & Co* in 2004 and set up the Accrediting Body for *Liberating Leadership* and *Pioneering Professional* in 2008, built on over 25 years' research and testing.

She has accredited over 100 practitioners to deliver the programmes and, for a fee, allows practitioners to brand the material in their own style – which they love. She is looking to grow this body of people so that other trainers, coaches, consultants and HR professionals have access to this powerful model to help them grow their own and their clients' businesses. The approach is attracting coaches all over the world – it works wherever you are.

"Our mission is to help every leader on the planet make developing their people their #1 priority."

Ali is a mentor, coach and practitioner of the profound *Insights Discovery®* system, Master NLP practitioner and member of the Association for Coaching. Having coached over 500 leaders she has a reputation for deep, delivering dramatic performance improvements.

ali@alistewartandco.com

www.alistewartandco.com

https://www.linkedin.com/in/alistewartandco/

https://twitter.com/alistewartandco

https://www.facebook.com/alistewartandco/

# Know Thyself

## Lorna Reeves

As I sit at my desk on a sunny Thursday afternoon, looking out over the Thames, I should be feeling fired up, positive and energised; I've gotten through my to do list, mailbox is almost clear, actions from my last three meetings completed.

I'm winning, right?

Wrong, I can feel fury and frustration rising in me. Every email I'm getting says something like *Please can we clarify ...* or *How should I go about?*

It gets worse, I can hear my staff chatting about a task and they are not on the right track, not even in the field next to the right track! Way off piste!

I get a piece of work from the team, completed – but it's not correct, or at least not what I expected. The tension is growing, how can they be getting it so wrong and then it hits me.

Maybe it's not them, perhaps it's me.

Cue *Ah-ha* music, coupled with dramatic camera zoom.

This is the moment that it occurred to me that perhaps my style is not synergistic with that of my team, perhaps my way of doing things, the assumptions I have made about others' understanding and ability and the way they work are not correct. This is the moment I decided to understand more about myself and my way of leadership, in order to understand others in my team and my customers in a bid to get more and better from our working relationship.

## Who are you?

Many of you will have under taken some kind of personality testing in the past, whether that be as part of your own development or in application for jobs/roles, but it is important that firstly, you find a testing that you like, secondly one you understand. If Myers- Briggs works for you then great, but there are many other types of testing and wording of the results. This will help you understand you and your personality. Get something done today. There are many free options online or pay a couple of dollars and the paid version will prove a lot more insightful.

It is interesting to note that as our careers grow and change, so do we. The personality type (Myers-Briggs), personality colour (360°) or letter combination (DiSC) you identified with seven years ago, even 18 months ago, may not be the same now.

Do this piece of reflective work regularly, perhaps once every year to 18 months. Check in with yourself.

Whilst your core values, the things you hold dearest, are unlikely to change, your style, patience and even your energy sources will. Things in your personal life will affect your work persona; changes with partners, children, houses or if your commute changes, all can affect the way in which you function at work. Even a shift in morale in the company or organisation you work for, may change your perspective and as such what you hold as important in the workplace.

## How do you?

When you have received your results, read them. Don't just skim the summary, really read them. Read them aloud, there's nothing like hearing your own voice describing yourself to really make it sink in. Next, be brave and discuss the results, discuss them with someone close to you, ask them, "Does this sound like me?" Also discuss them with someone at work, someone who's opinion you value.

Once you have really ingested your summary, read the descriptions of your polar opposite. How do they differ? Where can you see obvious clashes and when you read, listen to your body, there will be physical responses to some of the characteristics of the opposite personality type. As simple as rolling your eyes with frustration, to feeling your blood start to boil. Notice these feeling and remind yourself, this is not personal, they are valid characteristic but they just aren't yours.

These characteristics also bring a yin to your yang; without the antithesis to ourselves in a team or group setting we can miss opportunities, miss risk or even get into hot water. Observe where your profile weaknesses are and how your opposite fills these and vice versa. Take a look at the other types too and read around the others.

Most importantly, take out a note book and think about how you like to communicate? How do you like to function? Your personality test will probably include notes on this too.

Now have a think about your polar opposite, how might they prefer to work, function, process and communicate? Chances are it with be the exact flip of yours.

## What does this look like in reality?

I sat back after writing my reflections, reading and re-reading and noticed that I very much fitted my personality type, I am a fast moving, action taker, I like decisions to be made quickly, I prefer to communicate with short, concise sentences. I like to have the information presented clearly, with no spin, to enable me to balance risks quickly, make a decisions and move on. I work at 100 miles an hour and expect everyone else to keep up.

I realised this put me at risk of not looking at a problem and its solutions from all angles, this could be a vulnerability.

I noted I cut pleasantries and *forum discussions* out of my communications which could make other personality types feel silenced, stifled and unheard.

I saw my decisions were less creative and more factual and this was not always the best way and could be lacking.

I now saw why my staff were not *hearing me*, had to ask further questions and were getting things wrong, in my eyes – we were not communicating effectively. I was not speaking their language, in a way they preferred to hear it.

## In practice

Now you understand yourself, that's great! You can start to adapt your message delivery, you can start to adjust your style to assist others in understanding you, perhaps that is being less assertive and allowing time for questions and clarification or becoming more assertive to make decisions in a team of *thinkers*, in order to get your business to operate more effectively.

The next step is to have your staff understand themselves and be open to sharing the results in order to learn as a group. This might not be the entire staff, perhaps your own team and direct reports.

My staff all took the same test as me and I was first to share, I took the results, personalised them and gave them each a copy.

I included a section entitled, *How I like to communicate*. As I looked around the room, my teams' light bulbs went off. It was like they finally understood me. Equally on sharing their results, I realised that I was the only one of my personality type in the team, it also helped them understand each other and where miscommunication was occurring, predominately was message-delivery-failure.

Either failing to deliver in a way that ensures the person understands and really hears, or interpretation from their own personality type's bias, leading to misinterpretation and the message landing incorrectly.

In short:

- Learn about you and yourself
- Spend time learning about others, especially your opposite
- Encourage your team to learn about them
- Share your joint learnings
- Pause from time to time to reflect on your communication style and the receiving audience
- Rinse and repeat every 18 month or so.

## Know thyself to know others

Fundamentally, we as humans want to be heard, truly heard and understood. Wherever in life we can make this easier will only ever improve happiness, productivity and desire to do better. What more could you want from your team?

To know yourself and know others, you will not only reduce your own frustrations but earn respect and trust from your staff and them with each other as ensure they communicate with empathy, from a place of understanding – leading to faster and greater success.

*"To know thyself is the beginning of wisdom' - Socrates*

## Resources

- https://discpersonalitytesting.com/
- https://www.psychometrics.com/assessments/psychometrics-360/
- https://www.myersbriggs.org/home.htm?bhcp=1

* Other personality tests are available, please research to find one to suit you and your business

## About Lorna Reeves

Lorna Reeves, founder of the UK's only dedicated LGBT+ Wedding Planning service, has taken her leadership skills from 15 years in *Forensic Services* for *Metropolitan Police*, running Crime Scene teams and later the Laboratory team, motivating and driving the team towards targets and business objectives within public sector parameters. Teams of anywhere between 15 and 200 people were led by Lorna and her demanding yet understanding style.

Lorna has taken her ability to co-ordinate large numbers of people towards a common goal, her attention to minute detail and contracts, procurement experience to create her Wedding Planning company.

*MyOhMy Weddings*, strives to make the wedding planning journey enjoyable and stress free for its customers whilst Lorna, works hard to make positive change in the Wedding Sector for LGBT+ couples, encouraging same-sex couples in marketing and gender-neutral booking processes and training staff at venues and within suppliers in unconscious bias and how they can better serve the LBGT+ community.

www.myohmyweddings.com

lorna.reeves@myohmyweddings.com

Twitter @myohmyweddings

Facebook: www.facebook.com/myohmyweddings

Instagram: www.instagram.com/myohmyweddings

# Growth Mindset Of A Leader

## Kunal Dattani, Savan Dattani and Keval Dattani

*"Leadership is a mindset that shifts from being a victim to creating results. Any one of us can demonstrate leadership in our work and within our lives." Rob S. Sharma*

As entrepreneurs, mindset is a subject that is close to our hearts. Certainly, without a growth mindset, we wouldn't be in a position to speak to you on the topic today. The right mindset is what has helped us take our beard grooming brand, *Mo Bro's,* from a £750 investment and products created in a bedroom, to a seven-figure company with customers in 78 countries. And it's what is going to help you achieve your ambitions.

In this article, we're going to talk about the growth mindset that leaders need to reach their personal and professional goals.

But, first of all, what is mindset?

Mindset is defined as *the established set of attitudes held by someone.* These attitudes can differ depending on who you're discussing mindset with but, to our mind — based on our own personal and business development journey — they are mental toughness, core values, vision, authenticity and gratitude.

By focussing on, and working to improve, these five key areas of your life, you'll be able to maximise your leadership potential.

## Mental Toughness

Mental toughness is described by the speaker and author, Steve Siebold, as *having the ability to work hard and respond resiliently to failure and adversity… the inner quality that enables individuals to work hard and stick to their long-term passions and goals.*

We've found that even in the toughest of situations, you can persevere if you have the right mindset.

While we didn't know it at the time, our mental toughness was built as kids and probably inherited from our parents.

In the 1970's, our parents were expulsed from Uganda to the United Kingdom with only £20 to live on. Dad worked 18 hours a day, 7 days a week as the sole breadwinner — machine operator by day, Del Boy by night. It meant we didn't grow up with much in the way of material goods. We managed on 20p a day lunch money, shared toys and clothes, and never experienced the joys of a family holiday for 18 years.

Looking back, the hardships and adversity our family experienced were a blessing in disguise. They gave us the drive, determination and focus to be successful in life.

Our hardships aren't unique. Everyone in their life at some point will experience tough times, failure or adversity. It's what you do with those experiences that will improve your mindset.

Take your negative experiences and turn them into positives. Use them as fuel to drive you towards your goals.

## Knowing your core values

Core values are described as *a principle or belief that a person or organization views as being of central importance.*

We firmly believe that leadership starts within. Only by understanding your core values can you make a positive difference in your own life and to contribute to a larger cause. Values are the guiding principles in our lives. They are a part of us and they highlight what we stand for.

When you stay true to your core values you experience true fulfillment.

Our core values are health, ambition and honesty.

Your own values may differ but they can be found in the same way. We say *found* because core values aren't plucked out of thin air. You need to discover them.

You can do this by asking yourself three questions:

- What values are essential to your life?
- What values represent your primary way of being?
- What values are essential to supporting your inner self?

Your values may change over-time, with age and life experience. You might have three core values or ten. It doesn't matter. What matters is that you honour them. We find this easier to do when value statements are attached to each value. For example:

- Health — to live well, eat well and exercise to live a life full of happiness, energy and good mental health.

It's a simple step, but it gives a clarity to values that makes them easier to stick by.

## Vision

*"Good business leaders create a vision, articulate the vision, passionately own the vision, and relentlessly drive it to completion." - Jack Welch, Former CEO, General Electric*

One thing that unites great leaders always is their set vision. When *Amazon* went public in 1997, its founder, Jeff Bezos, wrote a letter to shareholders that gave indications of his long-term vision.

"We believe that a fundamental measure of our success will be the shareholder value we create over the long term," he wrote.

"We will continue to make investment decisions in light of long-term market leadership considerations rather than short-term profitability considerations or short-term Wall Street reactions."

Throughout the letter, Bezos talks about the plan for the long-term. It's was a different way of thinking about ecommerce at the time, but it helped *Amazon* succeed where so many internet companies of the time failed. *AOL, Lycos* and *Netscape,* for example, are all long gone, while *Amazon* is one of the biggest companies in the world.

A vision gives you the mental clarity to pursue your personal and professional goals.

Our vision has always been to make an impact within this world. That vision drives us to grow a sustainable business and earn enough money to secure our futures. From there, we can improve the lives of others.

All great leaders have visions that they believe in; whether it's to be financially free, to be known as a successful entrepreneur, or solve a world problem.

When you create a vision that you believe in, it becomes easier to improve your mindset. And the shift in mindset leads to more positive and actionable activities within your business.

For us, our vision has given us the clarity to prioritise daily activities. We've been able to extend this to employees within the business and create an environment where everyone contributes to something they believe in.

## Authenticity

We once read a quote about authenticity being a key ingredient to becoming a successful entrepreneurial leader. We couldn't agree more.

Authenticity helps to build lasting relationships in your personal and business lives. And there is no greater to way to be authentic than to be yourself.

In business, people often expect you to act a particular way or talk in a certain manner, but playing to stereotypes will only take you so far. People have a natural, subconscious ability to spot a lack of authenticity and any hint that you're not genuine will only serve to alienate them.

### Don't be afraid to be yourself

Authenticity allows you to have a realistic perception of reality, which creates a clear environment for you to continue with your daily activities.

## Gratitude

Gratitude is a much-favoured topic of ours and has had the most profound effect on our success. We believe that gratitude essentially starts within yourself. It's important to recognise your achievements and be thankful of the qualities you have.

Our biggest achievement was in May 2017, when we secured the largest *Dragons' Den* investment for two years. Initially, we never took time to reflect on what we had achieved.

In fact, it took almost two weeks to acknowledge the success.

However, it served as a lesson. Since then, we've taken the time to celebrate and be grateful for the opportunity. And it's given us the motivation to strive for more of those moments. Essentially, it's lead to better growth of the business.

In business, without gratitude, teams can start to disintegrate, culture can weaken and work can become stagnated and unattractive. Therefore, it's important to recognise that gratitude is a mechanism that powers positive leadership.

Particularly within the team you're leading, a simple appreciation can inspire others to develop and grow and feel motivated to achieve more with you.

Gratitude also extends to your customers. Letting customers know that you appreciate them is one of the best ways to achieve long-term brand loyalty.

## About the Mo Bros

Keval, Kunal and Savan Dattani are British-born entrepreneurs and founders of *Mo Bro's*, a leading mens grooming product retailer.

*Mo Bro's* was established in 2014 after the brothers discovered a gap in the market and a shortage of suitable beard and moustache products during a *Movember* challenge.

Starting with £750, the brothers have grown *Mo Bro's* into a seven-figure business that serves over 300,000 bearded brothers with a business based on, fun, brotherly love and a genuine passion for great beards.

*Mo Bro's* products are available in over 78 countries and sold in major retailers including *Next, Debenhams* and *ASOS*. They have been featured on *Dragons' Den* securing one of the highest offers of investments to date. *Mo Bro's* have reached an audience of over 125 million globally and attracted media coverage from the likes of *BBC, Telegraph* and the *Independent*. Most recently they have formed partnerships with the *PayPal, Amazon* and the Department for International Trade.

In 2018, *Mo Bro's* were awarded the best retailer of the year at the *Leicester Business Awards*. They were also runner-up in *PayPal's International Award* at Richard Branson's *Virgin VOOM 2018*.

www.mobros.co.uk

Kunal Dattani - www.linkedin.com/in/kunaldattani

Keval Dattani - http://www.linkedin.com/in/kevaldattani

Savan Dattani - http://www.linkedin.com/in/savandattani

# Motivating The Masses: Overcoming The Resignation And Reluctance In Your Leadership

**Daniel Browne**

According to HBR and other research, positive emotions foster greater engagement, creativity and performance. And while leaders realise this, few leaders are good at dealing with the negative emotions.

In real life we can't always be positive so we must learn to deal with the negative. We tend to ignore or suppress negative emotions, we are taught from an early age that displays of negative emotions are unacceptable. As a result, negative emotions often remain under the surface in the workplace and can build up.

You can walk into any office where there is a toxic build-up of negative emotions and you will know that this company's performance will not be at is most effective or could even go downhill.

This article outlines the negative factors of leadership that one needs to overcome in order to motivate people. If you can overcome these then you will be able to make great cultural transformations as a leader. The ability to understand, overcome and transform these emotions - effectively turning lead into gold - is a great skill to cultivate to be an excellent leader.

I was a bright ambitious student studying at University College London, determined to make the most of the opportunities available to me. I wanted the full experience. I joined as many clubs, societies and sports teams as I could fit in my calendar and I had an active social life. I loved university.

I sought as many positions of leadership that I could, knowing that this would enhance my prospects for a good job in engineering or business. I was a committee member in the engineering society and president of the *African Caribbean* society. It was fun. I got to organise and work with a great team, I undertook things I had no idea how to do such as putting on a fashion show. I loved making decisions and taking responsibility. This was the birth of a budding leader.

After University I continued this leadership at work and by joining volunteer organisations where I had the pleasure to thrive as a leader.

But after a few years I noticed that leadership became less fun over time. The work load increased, and it seemed that I had to do everything. My teams seemed less and less co-operative. Over time I became exasperated, complaining and resigned. On the surface I was still the nice guy that everyone liked but underneath I felt less unappreciated and put upon - the mug that took on everything.

I stopped raising my hand for leadership opportunities. I've been there done that I told myself. At the same time, I resented being lead or managed by others. I became smart and smug like a stubborn old man thinking I knew best, determined never to be taken advantage of again.

I wasn't going to be the person that everyone got to do things again. However deep down inside I was unfulfilled. There was a sadness, regret, resentment and the dull yearning of an unfulfilled leader. I had become the burnt out, reluctant leader.

At the time I didn't understand the symptom of *Leadership Reluctance and Resignation.*

This is when I discovered the 2Rs, the key emotional and thought patterns that kill off motivation and leadership.

## Reluctance and Resignation

Initially reluctance and resignation seem to be purely negative however they both have psychological function. They serve to protect the ego from upset and disappointment. They are helpful to a degree, but they often come from a misaligned perspective on life. Being able to recognise and effectively deal with reluctance and resignation is very useful to reinvigorate leadership in any organisation.

## Reluctance

*Reluctance* shows up in leadership as the unwillingness to take on new projects or accept new responsibilities.

The reluctant leader is capable of leadership but avoids taking on responsibility. As in my story, where once they were willing to take on new projects, over time they shy away from leadership.

There are a variety of external and internal factors that can contribute to this. The external factors include:

- Having an unsupportive work environment from senior leadership and management to an unsupportive or reluctant team.

- Having a work environment where the culture of delegation is more about dumping work on other people, or where *leader* is a code word for being someone that ends up cleaning up the mess.

Internal factors stem from perceptions of world and others that are not true in objective reality which cause issues in communication. For example, if the leader grew up being the responsible one in life and learned that controlling others is the best way to get results, they find this strategy doesn't work with people who don't like to be controlled.

There is a psychological utility to leadership reluctance. The underlying function of reluctance is your ego saying, "I was burnt or taken advantage of before, I used more energy than I got back, I won't be taken advantage of again."

This is in response to negative past experiences. Perhaps you became stressed to the point of burnout. Perhaps you felt betrayed by a team member or perhaps you were taken advantage of.

## Resignation

A team of bright young managers from among the leading ecommerce companies joined a new division within a large retailer. They were charged with creating an ecommerce business within the original company a traditional retailer. The new team were enthusiastic and highly talented, however there was resentment from the rest of the company. The new division experienced subtle push back on all proposals, there was a huge resistance to change and no matter how hard the new team worked they couldn't get things through at the rate of progress required to make the start-up division successful. After a year the energy and excitement in the division had all but died, the team had gone from frustrated to resigned; staff turnover increased. The talented people left for greener pastures that appreciated their talents.

Resignation is the key killer of business. While reluctance can be circumvented by finding another leader, resignation is more toxic.

Let's understand the ego's role of resignation. Like reluctance, resignation is an energy saving mechanism. It is our ego telling us to give up on that goal, nothing will really change so there is no point in attributing any energy in pursuit of a goal. The goal of resignation is to protect us from expending any energy on something that, in our perceptions will not change or will not make a difference. (Remember, these are subconscious thoughts that are impacting us).

Resignation sounds like: "There are no opportunities for me in this company, so I'll save my hopes and dreams and give the bare minimal energy. I'm not going to expend energy into something that won't work out". People feel they have no voice and their voice makes no difference. They become angry and then give up.

## Dealing with Reluctance and Resignation

Before we can impact our organisations, it is helpful to address where we have reluctance or resignation regarding our own roles. When we have done that for ourselves it is easier motivate others. Trying to motivate a resigned crowd is like a *David Brent* scene in an office. You'll come across as an unconvincing motivator trying to cheer people up to act. It doesn't work.

## How to work with your own leadership reluctance

If you are experiencing reluctance or want to avoid it, inquire into what your needs are as a leader. What conditions do you require for you to want to engage as a leader? Do you need a great team? Do you need fun? A serious committed team? What will you get out of leading?

Consider if past experiences contributed to your feelings of reluctance. Explore what the source of reluctance could be.

What was missing that would have stopped the development of reluctance?

### Overcoming resignation for yourself

To overcome your own resignation, explore the resignation. What are you actually *resigned* about? What do you feel is hopeless?

Then look at what is resignation or reluctance trying to protect you from? Disappointment? Expending unnecessary energy? Is your viewpoint a realistic analysis of the situation? How else could you get the result you want? What have you not explored or considered?

### How to motivate others

We can usually tell what's going on just by walking around the company. You can feel the energy in the room. For major concerns a coach or a specialist in team management and leadership will be able to facilitate an intervention. However, we can address this with team members on an individual basis or with a group. It requires being direct, sensitive but not being afraid to go into uncomfortable territory.

We can use the same inquiry above for the group either holding an individual session or as a team exercise.

### Creating a culture to turn around
### reluctance and resignation

There are ways to engineer a culture that is proof against the reluctance and resignation:

- Create a culture where leadership is rewarded and doesn't just mean more work.

- Understand what leaders get out of leading? What growth and development are available for leaders and their teams?

- How are people acknowledged or rewarded for their time and energy?

- Have a system for feedback to be received. This ensures that resignation doesn't get a chance to build up.

Resignation and reluctance can happen to any company. Being aware of how to turn it around will prevent toxic negativity build up.

## About Daniel Browne

An expert in productivity, performance and wellbeing, Daniel Browne will show you how to be more productive, industrious and efficient.

Daniel started his career working in an investment bank in the city and has worked in extremely demanding jobs for most of his career in finance and strategy consulting.

After a few years, working over 12 hours a day (often working through the night, sacrificing weekends and a social life) started to take its toll.

Daniel was exhausted and really concerned about his wellbeing. There had to be a more efficient way to perform well at work and still have a life.

Daniel started researching alternative methods of performance improvement. He studied everything from mediation, yoga, Tai Chi, neuroscience, relaxation techniques and even hypnotherapy. He then created a program designed to meet the needs of people working in demanding jobs with little time to spare for anything else.

This was the beginning of the book. *The Energy Equation: How to be a top performer without burning yourself out.*

Daniel now specialises in helping leaders and teams get better results by elevating their level of performance and leadership.

www.danielebrowne.com

https://www.linkedin.com/in/danielbrowne1

db@danielebrowne.com

# The Impostor Syndrome:
# How It Manifests, What You Can Do About It

## Suparna Malhotra

A year ago I was asked to write an article on the topic of the *Impostor Syndrome*. Until that point my only reference to an impostor was the glamorous character, Mike Ross on the TV show *Suits*. In case you are not familiar, Mike Ross poses as an associate lawyer in a top NYC law firm, having brains and a photographic memory, but not the qualifications.

Mike Ross is not the kind of impostor we will be speaking about here. We will talk about what is known as the *Impostor Syndrome*. It was officially coined by two psychologists in 1978, Pauline Clancy and Suzanne Imes in their paper entitled, *The Impostor Phenomenon in High Achieving Women: Dynamics and Therapeutic Intervention*. (Clancy, Imes 1978)

The paper described the *Impostor Phenomenon* as a feeling that occurs in high achieving women in who were unable to internalise their successes, they credited them to luck or to chance and felt they were not deserving of the accolades or credit they received. These individuals feared that eventually others would see through their mask. They attributed this to certain familial dynamics and societal expectations.

Earlier in the year while planning one of my workshops (funnily enough, on the *Impostor Syndrome*, for successful female leaders), I suddenly doubted my own credibility. Despite the successes and highs in my career, and an upcoming event at *Google*, a niggling sensation rose up questioning what right I had to be there.

At a pinnacle moment of my success I was standing in doubt.

There is a famous quote by an unknown author who said, "I'm always worried I'm not smart enough to have *impostor syndrome*".

There is a silver lining to experiencing the *impostor syndrome* - this only really happens to you if you're successful. It is when we reach great heights, when we can look down from the point we are standing and feel the vertigo. Many actors, successful writers, even politicians go through this. Yes, it shouldn't be a surprise, as far as politicians go!

Comedienne, Tina Fey famously said, "The beauty of the *Impostor Syndrome* is you vacillate between extreme egomania and a complete feeling of: 'I'm a fraud! Oh God, they're on to me! I'm a fraud!' So you just try to ride the egomania when it comes and enjoy it, and then slide through the idea of fraud."

What's more, even the legendary poet, Maya Angelou felt, "I have written eleven books, but each time I think, 'Uh oh, *they're* going to find out now. I've run a game on everybody, and they're going to find me out.'"

Over the summer I worked with a young lady who was in charge of social impact and human rights in the supply chain for a renowned brand. A stretch job for her, in her own words, but in line with her ambitious values.

The environment where she worked was highly male dominated. She found herself sitting in meetings, knowing exactly what the solutions were, yet not speaking up for fear of being judged.

She found herself become increasingly nervous around the various stakeholders, particularly in a group settings. As a result, she felt her confidence waning.

During our session she identified the thoughts that held her back as following:

- If I were smarter, I would not be nervous
- I was at the right place, at the right time to get this job

These are powerful statements and my client believed them to be true. She spent all her time and effort trying to prove she deserved the role. This is what psychologist Carol S Dweck has termed *a fixed mindset* (Dweck, 2008). A fixed mindset is where you see yourself as never being able to surpass where you are now.

Carol believes that this can be changed. That those struggling with *impostorism* can train them-selves to shift from a fixed mindset to a growth mindset. A person who sits in the fixed mindset, in Carol's definition, believes that failure is the limit of their abilities. Those in the *growth mindset* see failure as an opportunity to grow.

The client and I discussed which mindset she preferred to be in. I asked her to recap her career history to date. When looking at the time line she had illustrated in her notebook she realised that all the jobs she'd had were due to her achievements and because she had said yes to opportunities and new challenges.

My client was struck by just how much of a driving force she had been in landing her position. She also began to accept that she was smart, she knew what she was talking about and what she did not she was capable of learning.

The acceptance of these facts alone, and declaring her vision of how she wanted it to be with her colleagues, and stakehold-ers, she was filled with a renewed inspiration to speak up in meetings.

One thing to remember when any of these feelings creep up is that you are not alone. The thoughts you're having of not knowing as much as the other ... they have them too. I've worked with numerous successful leaders in *FTSE 50* companies, who find it hard to own their successes (men and women). Often it is those who are the most accomplished and knowledgeable who realise they do not know anything at all.

The great news is that these feelings can be shifted. Here are some ways you can do this:

1. **Write an email:** Write an email to yourself listing out all your accomplishments so you have them as a reminder for your next role. This great tip came from an ex-colleague and friend of mine. It's amazing how quickly we can forget what and where we were.

2. **Past successes:** This I learned from my very patient tennis instructor. He asked me to play back just what I had done and repeat it. Accept a beginner's mindset and just keep practicing. If you have just completed a big project that was received well and you think, ah I'll never be able to re-peat that, just think about it in the same way as my tennis coach tried to teach me to serve.

3. **Two voices:** We all have two voices in our heads. One that encourages us and believes in us, the other wants to hold us back. Become aware of these voices and decide which one you wish to listen to.

4. **Ask your friends or colleagues:** Your friends, family and colleagues see you as you are. Ask them how they see you. It is also helpful to remember that mistake is just a teacher in disguise. Recognise this.

5. **Focus on the beneficiaries:** We feel like a fraud when we are focused on ourselves. You will find that when you experience this your ego has a role to play. Think about the value you provide to others, through the work you do.

For example, my client had to focus on the people she was helping in her new role. Taking herself out of the equation and focusing on the value and who it's for is a great way to bring back confidence.

6. **Values Affirmation exercise:** Take 30 minutes to write about what matters to you and why. Studies have shown that doing this improves performance and can increase confidence.

7. **Talk about it:** Talking about your *dark* secret to someone you trust will immediately reduce its grip on you. For one, the person you trust won't see it. Secondly, being able to say it out loud reduces its effect almost immediately.

8. **Acceptance:** Accept where you are and that you got there for a reason. Successes can be a direct result of your latest project, it can be through your network, it can be because you said yes. None of these mean you are any less deserving of it.

9. **Hire a Coach/Mentor:** Perhaps because I am one, I see the benefits in seeking outside help. When we reach a certain stage, we can benefit from bringing our best selves to the table by ridding ourselves of limitations. A coach can help with this. They will see you objectively and will hold you to your highest standards.

10. **Stay in the growth mindset:** Always see life as an adventure, with learning and failure as the perfect tool for your growth. Remember that our brains are constantly growing and stretching and so are we.

You are now equipped with some ideas of how to negate self doubt and feelings of being a fraud. Something I remind the leaders who work with me is that in order for them to lead they need to inspire trust. To inspire trust from others, they need to trust themselves. Trust yourself to stay in a growth mindset. When in doubt, seek help. Do what is necessary to bring yourself back to solid ground and lead from your heart.

# References

- Clancy. P. and Imes. S. (1978). *The Impostor Phenomenon in High Achieving Women: Dynamics and Therapeutic Intervention.* Georgia State University

- Dweck. C. (2008). *Mindset.* Random House, USA.

## About Suparna Malhotra

Suparna Malhotra coaches professionals from *FTSE 100* companies, and across a variety of industries including global FMCGs, finance and technology. She runs an executive coaching and training practice in London, UK and has been highly commended by *Forbes*.

Twitter: @thesuparnaway

www.linkedin.com/in/suparnamalhotra

www.suparnaway.com

## Meaning and Purpose

**Spiritual, values, ethics,
moral behaviours, legacy, generativity,
rehearsing the future**

# A Different Kind Of Grit!

## Dr Tina Allton

Being a young girl growing up in West Africa in the 1970's certainly gives you a different kind of grit!

*Wikipedia* explains grit as: '... *Grit* in psychology is a positive, non-cognitive trait based on an individual's perseverance of effort combined with the passion for a particular long-term goal or end state (a powerful motivation to achieve an objective). This perseverance of effort promotes the overcoming of obstacles or challenges that lie on the path to accomplishment and serves as a driving force in achievement realisation.'

Whilst the dictionary defines it as 'firmness of character; indomitable spirit.'

### Creating A Win Through The Moments Of Correction

If you are like me, you probably have been corrected before, perhaps in your childhood or even your adult life, and yet it still is one of the most uncomfortable truths anyone can ever face. It is not an exciting thing to be given any form of correction, however small, and yet it is true that correction provides us with many opportunities to work on who we are, to help us to grow and become better people. It also provides us with the process to not just develop but also to mature.

If you have ever seen a boxing match, they each prepare, train for endless months in advance and each moment their training comes with a level of correction from their coach. Would it be a bad thing to give correction at such a crucial time as a during a match? One can argue so. However, when you consider it, in the moment of correction, when given, taken and applied, the boxer can be assured of winning the match.

**Ground Rule:** Never underestimate the correction from your mentor - they correct you and most importantly affirm you because they have your best interest at heart and ultimately you want to be where they have already been. The correction from a mentor is effectively sowing the seeds of who you can be, long before you become that person.

**Action Point:** Always ask for feedback and correction - it makes all the difference.

## Allowing The Plan To Go Off Script

Like most of us, we all have made plans at some point in our lives. Often times, we may well judge ourselves too hard when our plans fail or when they go totally *off script*, as I call it.

I remember going to see my family doctor for a routine check-up, in November 2017. A few seconds into the appointment, my doctor tells me that my check-up was actually not due for some time. Rather than making me feel stupid for wasting her time, she proceeded to asking how I was.

Generally, I am very healthy. Having a daughter with diabetes for the last 17 years has meant that the entire family has come round to eating healthily. But I mention some mild pain. Shortly after explaining my symptoms to my doctor, she stops me and tells me straight in the face, "I think you may be exhibiting the symptoms of bowel cancer."

Nothing could have prepared me for that news or indeed what followed next. Within 24 hours I was having various blood tests, scans of all sorts and I probably saw the most number of doctors and specialists that I have ever seen in my entire life!

Months of various tests continued until finally in February 2018, I was given the all-clear of any cancer. Now during these times, no plan was needed except the plan to live and see my children grow up.

**Ground Rule:** Planning is good, but sometimes we have to embrace the fact that it is perfectly okay to allow our plans to go totally off schedule, because it is in those moments of flexibility that one gets to discover what is truly important. Often times, you find yourself again, better shaped and ready to advance!

**Action Point:** Next time you find your plans going off script, do not fret, it is all part of the plan! Delegate whenever you can.

## Purpose And Process

There is a lot of hype these days about chasing your dreams, follow your purpose and achieve it at all cost! What is often overlooked is the fact that to achieve those dreams and in pursuing that purpose, one must follow a process – that series of actions that will need to be taken in order to arrive at the desired end

One 48 year-old gentleman, married with three children, always wanted to be in aviation. From a much young age, his parents encouraged him to pursue his dreams. What he hadn't been taught was: it is one thing to have a dream and another to have a process in place to achieve those dreams.

Just like most of us, he had to start from very humble beginnings - the process of getting rejected many times, learning to pick himself back up again from discouragement - before finally getting qualified to get into aviation school. Then, there were months of studying to pass the exams, before securing a scholarship to study in Scotland.

Even the process of getting accustomed to harsh weather conditions nearly made him give up on that dream.

I remember speaking to him one very cold day, in December 2002, encouraging him to persist.

After that call I came to the stark realisation that every dream requires a process and most of the time you will need to make many sacrifices along the way to achieve your dream. You will also have to learn the art of bouncing back when you get knocked down. And you will need to have someone to keep you accountable along the way for those unplanned moments when you desperately want to give up because it all feels too overwhelming.

My friend today is one of the most sought-after aviation officers, not just in Ghana or Africa, but across the world! Imagine if he had given up!

**Ground Rule:** Without a process, you lose your purpose and focus, but at the end of the process, you get the rewards!

**Action Point:** For every goal you set, identify the process required to achieve these, make a commitment to yourself and remain accountable to someone to the exception of yourself.

## Control your Environment

One of the key things that I always recommend to leaders and business owners is controlling the people in your environment, specifically, the kind of influence or impact they are making on your life, your business, and your beliefs.

Motivation expert, Jim Rohn puts it much better. "You are the sum of the five people that you hang out with."

Of course you don't get to choose your family, but you do get to choose who can become your friend, and subsequently, who gets to be in your environment.

In a recent podcast on *Medium.com*, David Burkus, said that your life is impacted by more the five closest people and in more ways than expected. He cited a study by Nicolas Chistakis and James Fowler, who examined data sets from the *Framingham Heart Study,* one of the longest running health studies, started in 1948.

They discovered that the health of the participants was certainly affected by family members and friends. For example, when your friend becomes obese, you have a 45% likeliness of becoming obese also within two to four years. Likewise, if a friend of your friend becomes obese you still had a 20% chance of becoming obese and you don't even have to know that friend!

Drawing on data spanning over 30 years they looked at issues such as smoking, and found that you had a 69% of becoming a smoker too if you had a friend who smoked, if the friend of your friend was a smoker, you were still 29% likely to smoke too.

**Ground Rule:** In addition to your immediate network, understand that your social network also extends to people you connect with via social media platforms. It is therefore an imperative to carefully review your friends - and their friends too! Who is connected to you? And, are they influencing you for the best or increasing your chances of failure?

**Action Point:** Cut out anyone who does not influence or impact you positively, and remember to only go where you are celebrated not tolerated!

### Bugs in your ear

A *bad bug* in your ear can be a nuisance and most uncomfortable, they can be likened to the family member or friend who doesn't encourage you when you most need it, the same can be said at times for the challenges we face in life as business leaders.

On the other hand, the *good bug* can be likened to a mentor, who can see your strengths, motivate and inspire you, provide insights for growth, help you identify greater opportunities and hold you accountable.

I can confidently attribute my success to my mentors; my grandmother being my first, at age eight. She helped shape me to become the woman I am today. Over four decades on and I will not be without a mentor. Having a mentor puts a good bug in your ear and sets you up for success!

In 2012, a survey conducted by *MicroMentor.org* found that those who had mentoring increased their revenues by an average of 106%; those who didn't receive mentoring had an average increase of only 14%.

The important role of mentors is easy to see in popular culture. We can equally learn from history and some of the most famous how mentoring played a part in their success Plato was mentored by Socrates, Aristotle was the mentor of Alexander the Great. Even the most successful people have had a mentor. Warren Buffet was mentored by Benjamin Graham, and Marissa Myers is mentored by Larry Page.

You can also be inspired - and mentored - by role models. When American activist, Rosa Parks was arrested for refusing to give up her seat to a white passenger on a bus, her actions changed the world's attitude to racial prejudice, civil liberties and racial discrimination laws.

Malala Yousafzai won a Nobel Prize for human rights specifically, risking her own life for the right of girls to receive an education.

Dame Anita Roddick changed the way the world thought about testing cosmetics on animals.

Each in their own way, became a good bug in our ear, spurring us to think and act in more resourceful ways.

**Ground Rule:** A bug is only bad if it doesn't help you to grow. It is a no-brainer to realise that when you feel stuck, it is probably a good time to examine what type of bug have in your ear. It is safe to say that a great mentor is always going to be a good bug to have in your ear.

**Action Point:** Identify 2-3 people who have already been where you desire to get to, have similar values/culture you aspire to, someone who inspires and motivates you to no end, then go hang out where you are most like to meet them.

Build a relationship or ask a remarkable question so they will remember you and then ask to be mentored. You may well get a 'No', but guess what, you could equally get a 'Yes', because until you ask, the answer is always a NO!

## About Dr Tina Allton

Dr. Tina Allton is a global entrepreneur, keynote speaker, educational psychologist, and award-winning mentor spanning the international business, non-profit, medical, womens' empowerment, and global impact worlds. She holds an honorary doctorate (HC) in Humanities: Leadership.

Tina has co-founded six successful businesses over two decades and worked with over 5,000 entrepreneurs. She is Head of Global Expansion and CFO for *Empowering a Billion Women By 2020,* (EBW2020) a worldwide fintech and educational women empowerment platform. She is the High Commissioner to Ghana for the *World Business Angels* investment forum, CEO and co-founder of *Undefeeted. org,* a fast-growth diabetes nonprofit inspired by her daughter, and award winning business manager to one of London's most successful podiatric practices, *Circle Podiatry* (as well as loving wife and mother to four beautiful children).

As a sought-after speaker, Tina has spoken in 12 countries, and shared the stage with Sylvester Stallone, Al Pacino, Jermaine Jackson, Vanilla Ice and Michelle Mone, as well as business and thought leaders such as Dr. Nido Qubein, (Highpoint University, USA), Jay Abraham, Randi Zuckerberg and Ingrid Vanderveldt.

tina@tinaallton.com

https://www.linkedin.com/in/tinaallton/

https://twitter.com/tinaallton

http://www.tinaallton.com/

https://www.facebook.com/DrTinaAllton

https://www.facebook.com/tinaalltonofficial/

# What We Focus On, We Get More Of

## Alan Hester

Working with a wide cross-section of leaders and organisations, I have noticed something that is both surprising and common. People at all levels of an organisation spend most of their time on activities and concerns that have little or nothing to do with the most important goal they are employed to achieve.

Think about the average meeting, whether at team, management or board level, and the amount of time spent in a structured way on planning for achievement of our important goals and making decisions to help achieve them. Then compare this to time spent on routine updates on diaries, personality based issues or circular debates on immediate problems that fail to reach a conclusion or stimulate specific action.

Most of us would confidently say that we know what we are trying to achieve, and most of our organisations would proudly share with you their mission, vision or values. These goal and priority statements are often framed and can be seen hanging on the wall above reception, or adorning the cover of business plans or the home page of websites. We are happy to pronounce that the customer comes first or we are the employer of choice in our sector.

We have goals to be the best or do the best; ambitious targets to work towards and milestones to achieve on the way.

With the best of intentions however, reality can be very different. The framed picture above reception may say one thing but if our thoughts and actions say another then those noble aims will not reflect our reality. Experience shows that we are not what we say, we are what we do.

Much of our working day is spent on activities and behaviours that have nothing to do with the professed purpose of our organisation. Instead of thinking about what would take us forward we deal with what's in front of us. Instead of making the choices that will bring us closer to our goals we make choices based on expediency.

This is partly to do with life's knack of throwing us the unexpected – after all the former British Prime Minister Harold Macmillan, when asked what had been the most difficult aspect of the job, famously replied: 'Events, dear boy.'

We are all familiar with the experience of arriving at work with a list of things to achieve, then spending the whole day working incredibly hard only to find that we achieved none of them because *events* had taken over. There is always something more important to do than what we really want to do. At least that's often how it seems to a busy leader, juggling priorities, answering questions, making decisions and supporting or chasing colleagues. The problem is that what we see as important is typically not the most important thing in front of us; it may be the most visible, the most urgent or the most important to the person we are with, but it isn't the most important thing in helping us to achieve our goals.

We also, because we are human, spend an inordinate amount of time worrying about these things. I've written extensively about worry elsewhere, but would just like to throw in an idea here that is worth reflecting on: worry takes you backwards, but thinking takes you forwards.

What I mean by this is that endlessly worrying about smaller issues or imagining future problems can only reinforce our negativity by focussing on the problem; thinking on the other hand is the precursor to doing something about the problem, which means we are focussing instead on the solution. Thinking leads to planning, which in turn leads to action. What we focus on, we get more of.

The impact of this is clear but may be more far-reaching than we know. This is because our behaviour directly influences the behaviour of our colleagues. If we spend our time firefighting it sets the tone for everyone else too. Our habits become their habits and, whether we are leading a small team or a large organisation, we are creating a culture and culture is as I said earlier, not what we say but what we do. People form habits and as leaders we are no different, except that our habits become the habits of those who rely on us.

**What do we spend our time on?** This is a big and often discussed topic so I will limit myself to a few key areas to think (not worry!) about, and where a small change in our habits can make a significant difference to our results:

- Every interaction with colleagues, partners and clients is significant in achieving our purpose. The more time we waste on lower priority activity the more we delay success.

- The average manager spends 15% of their working week looking for things! This doesn't only waste your time but ropes other people in to the general air of panic and disorganisation.

- Structure, process and organisation never hurt anyone. I often reflect on the three simple rules for business the owner of a scrap metal dealership told me: "Simplicity, organisation and being fair to the customer." He and his team base their entire operation on those three principles.

- Decide on the most important thing to do today, and do it. When *events* get in the way, simply deal with the interruption and then get straight back into your priority without flitting between all the other less important distractions.

**What are we rewarding?** We need to reward the right behaviours. Every time we give feedback we are reinforcing our message so if we fail to recognise when someone does the right thing, we are missing a chance to show that doing the right thing is significant. Every time we reward the wrong behaviour we are reinforcing the wrong things.

One example of this is the tendency to spend all our time on *problem* people and to leave *good* performers alone. The *problem* person is rewarded by our time, attention, support, suggestions and encouragement – despite having achieved nothing of importance to our organisation. The *good* performer is neglected, perhaps notices the amount of focus their colleague is getting for the *wrong* behaviour and wonders why he or she is making so much effort; crucially, by missing out on your time, they are also not being stretched and challenged and you are potentially missing out on further contributions they could make.

This also applies to you! Make sure you reward yourself for being effective, not simply for being *busy*. Working late and feeling stressed is not a badge of honour but can be a sign that you are either not doing things right or are not doing the right things.

**What is important to us?** We will achieve what we decide to achieve. Genuine commitment will always win out over expediency. There are a few key behaviours here that we can helpfully understand and commit to:

- Decisions are much easier to make if they are based on a consistent purpose or goal rather than on what suits us at the time. If doing or not doing something takes us further towards our goal, we do it; if it takes us away from our goal we don't.

- Values are vital. Again, if something contradicts our values, we are best to find a way that reinforces them. Often, what is easy in the short term leads to difficulty later, while what is difficult now can make long term success more achievable.

**What is our *normal*?** Normal is what we do every day. You create the habits by which you personally work, and this creates the culture of your team.

I once banned the phrase, *I haven't got time* – none of us were allowed to use it to justify not taking something on. The result of this (apart from some temporary unpopularity of course) was that we were then forced into having a proper conversation about our priorities and workloads. It may be that I was asking people to do too much, or that they were doing things they shouldn't be doing.

It may be that we had to decide what was important, and do it. It was a great opportunity to focus our efforts on doing the important stuff. The more time we spend on the important things, the more we discuss them, the more we work through our challenges on the way to achievement, the greater our understanding of and commitment to our goals.

We can keep our focus where it is most effective by judging and measuring everything we do against our mission, vision and values. Plan it, discuss it, review it, argue about it. A good old-fashioned argument based on principles and goals can be incredibly useful; what is not helpful is conflict based on personal agendas, quick fixes or buck passing.

I know it's not new, but Bruce Tuckman's *team development cycle* is a great model at all levels of an organisation: real, values-based discussion (*Storming*) is essential if we are to arrive at clear processes and values (*Norming*), and the quality and consistency of these lead to great results (*Performing*).

What gets measured gets delivered. What we focus on, we get more of.

## About Alan Hester

Alan Hester is an international author and trainer specialising in management, leadership and personal development.

Alan has worked successfully with leadership teams and individual managers at all levels in a wide variety of industries and sectors spanning private, public and community organisations. His training is practical and flexible, working with organisations and individuals to help them to achieve their objectives.

Alan's book *Management Starts With You* (Robinson), described as 'a wise, honest and practical guide' for managers and leaders, is available in the UK, USA and fifteen other countries and has been translated into Chinese, Arabic and Greek.

His second book *Get Out Of Your Own Way* on personal success and improvement, was published by Robinson in 2018.

https://www.linkedin.com/in/alanhester1/

# What Human Beings Really Want That's Missing From Your Business Right Now

## Ryan Mathie

As a Personal Development Coach, I've worked closely with the full spectrum of humanity: from CEOs and Managing Directors at the top of the business world through to highly talented creatives such actors, musicians and artists and regular people struggling as partners and parents, sons and daughters, brothers and sisters.

Over a decade of inter-personal work, I've discovered that all my clients wanted something that they didn't actually know they wanted - transformation of their mindset – so they could create the specific results that they did know that they wanted - such as connected relationships and increased productivity in their careers and finances.

What if I told you that there was a way you could have the results you really want right now? Like more power, purpose and freedom? Excited? Well I'm going to share with you the five essential elements required to have all this in your personal and professional life.

As any coach knows, you can't give away what you don't already have. I'm able to promise more power, purpose and freedom because I've discovered and rediscovered this for myself in my own life.

But it wasn't always this way. My first 30 years in this life was a combination of fun and adventure in my personal life and one failure after the next professionally. I was trying to work out where I was headed but I had no clue what life was really all about. I had experienced conventional success, making money and accomplishments, but I *failed* to really feel *good* about what I was waking up to do every day.

Ever since I can remember up until 30, I was searching for something deeper with more purpose and meaning. I tried, failed, learned, tried again and repeated this struggle countless times.

I instinctively knew I would figure things out if I just kept going. But I won't lie, there were some really challenging days in my 20s while I stumbled around in the dark searching for the light.

Ten years ago, I experienced a defining moment. I had a profound personal experience walking through East London. I was having a familiar kind of argument with a girlfriend at that time. The kind of argument where she was wrong and I was right. However, for no apparent reason on this occasion I noticed a pattern. In a single moment, my whole life flashed in front of me. In all the arguments I had ever had the one consistent factor was me. Up until this moment I'd always thought it was *them* at fault. I begun to realise I'd been seeing life one way, from my own point of view and that there was a reality - a truth - that I'd never seen before.

The realisation was simultaneously devastating and truly transformational. This revelation literally blew my mind so much I thought I was going to pass out. I walked home alone, entered my house, walked into my bedroom and closed the door. In the minutes and hours that followed, I cried out the pain of 30 years of BS as I woke up to my *self.* Insight after insight hit me like crashing waves - about my life, my family, my relationships, my mistakes, things I had done that I was not proud of and how

I had been getting in my own way. Through all the tears, I began to feel awake for the first time in my entire life and something magical and very natural started to happen.

The next day I had real conversations with my family for what felt like the first time in my life. I opened up, shared and connected to them on a level that was so deep and so nurturing to my soul. My honesty created a safe space for them to open up too. Admittedly they were a bit freaked out by it all!

I contacted friends, colleagues and relationships from my past and finally started clearing up my part in things that happened that didn't work. I started cleaning up my entire life.

Chasing a career for money and status just didn't fit any longer. I wanted my life to count for something. Whatever I was discovering was so important that I wanted to go deeper, develop profoundly within myself and find ways to share it with others.

In the coming days, weeks, months and years I began to create my life versus being a reaction to it. I had never felt so powerful, purposeful and free in all my life.

What happened that day? What was the source of such a shift? What inner process occurred that led to such radical new results? I didn't have the words right away and that was OK – I just knew it felt right and that I was exactly where I needed to be.

It would take a few years and a huge amount if insight, training, development, growth, books, seminars and workshops before I would be able to effectively articulate the profound transformational experience that occurred that day.

Here are the *Five Essential Elements for Power, Purpose and Freedom* in your personal and professional life.

## 1. Spacious Awareness

This is also referred to as inner spaciousness, self-awareness, presence or as I like to refer to it – space.

When there is no space, we end up in survival mode, trapped in the internal dialogue of our minds. It righteously tells us what and who is wrong and identifies all the threats around us. Our brain is an expert survival machine. But the problem is we end up surviving threats that we make up in our mind. Our *mind-made reality* projects itself on to the world and we are completely unaware. We see life a certain way and defend ourselves from things that don't really exist. Sound familiar?

When there is space you are aware. You are able to *notice* the internal dialogue for what it is, an internal dialogue (versus something real). In this space you have the freedom to choose powerfully rather than reacting to life. You see things for what they are versus your story about them.

**Exercise:** Think of an area of your life where you feel upset, anxious, worried, stressed, angry or in any way disempowered. Slow down and notice the dialogue, notice the story, notice the *who's right* and *who's wrong*. Just slow right down and notice it.

## 2. Personal Integrity

When there is no personal integrity there is something in the back of our head, gnawing away at us. We *know* the truth and we *know* what works and what does not but we get caught up in justifying, excusing and turning a blind eye.

When there is a lack of personal integrity, circumstances around us just don't seem to work out that well.

When there is integrity there is clarity, you feel strong. You operate in life with your head held high. You are known for being reliable and you have a kind of honour with yourself. Personal integrity is just that; it is personal. And the more personal integrity you cultivate through honouring yourself to yourself the more freedom and power you will have to deal with everything life throws are you. There is no 100 per cent game here – just a commitment to holding yourself up as high as you can.

**Exercise:** Think of an area of your life where you know you lack personal integrity. Notice how it's impacting you. What would you need to do next to bring back a sense of honour for yourself to yourself?

## 3. Authenticity

When you are being inauthentic you are hiding, denying, pretending and covering up something. To be blunt, it feels horrible. We want to look good and be admired so much we are willing to play fake. However, what is more inspiring than a human being owning their humanity? We are not perfect, we are not robots, we don't always get it right and that's okay. Be you, don't pretend to be perfect.

**Exercise:** Think of an area of your life where you are pretending or covering up something. What does it feel like? How will the situation be in three, six and 12 months down the line if nothing changes? Is this how you really want to live? If you had the courage to bring authenticity to this area – what would that give you?

## 4. Responsibility

When there is a lack of responsibility you can perceive situations rigidly as black and white and right and wrong and attract disagreements, breakdowns, reasons, excuses, ineffectiveness and powerlessness. You can feel like the pinball in the machine of your own life. Power struggles are very frustrating because it really does look like it's *them* – all the other person's fault!

Responsibility brings power. You become bigger, taller, more alert, more awake and you see a way through any obstacle in front of you. This is an inspiring way to live.

**Exercise:** Where in your life are you playing the *blame game*? Where is it his/her/their fault? Try owning the whole thing, try coming at the situation being responsible for everything you are responsible for. Own your part completely. Now what?

## 5. Contribution

When there is a lack of contribution life is just all about *me* and getting caught up in minutia and dealing with small problems. Nothing wrong with focusing on the details but you are so much bigger than this. You are so powerful that the *me* game will always keep you small because the world is so much bigger that you.

Contribution to others brings immeasurable fulfillment. Why? Because at our core we all want to our life to count for something bigger and we want to make a difference.

The energy that gets tapped when we are up to something bigger and more meaningful in the world seems unlimited. Human beings tend to need a much bigger problem to solve to discover who we really are and what we're capable of.

**Exercise:** Consider something in the world that really matters to you – a truly big and meaningful problem. How could you get up each morning to solve that problem? If you need help answering, a useful place to start looking is here: *www.globalgoals.org*

If you just read through the exercises I encourage you to create the space and time you need to do the work. If not, let the questions percolate and work on you. It will feel uncomfortable and that's a sure sign that you are doing it right. Expansion is not comfortable.

Send me an email and let me know what happened and what you discovered *ryan@ryanmathie.com*

Here is what I would really like to leave you with. Over the last ten years, working with people from all walks of life, from all over the world – do you know what I have discovered? Beyond fear of confrontation and fear of the unknown, each and every single person I've worked with has unknowingly wanted the same things.

They wanted self-awareness, to live with personal integrity, to be authentic, responsible and to make a difference. Some of them needed showing the way, some of them needed obstacles cleared first and some of them just needed the permission.

## About the Author

Ryan Mathie, 39, was born in the small town of Bellshill in North Lanarkshire, Scotland. He is the great nephew of the late Sir Matt Busby, CBE, KCSG who was a Scottish football player and manager of Manchester United.

At 20, Ryan moved to London where he lived for 18 years, before moving to Tunbridge Wells, Kent, in the idyllic southeast corner of the UK.

Ryan's expertise developed over the last 10 years after a profound transformative experience while walking through the streets of Bethnal Green, London. He went on to work with one of the world's leading organisations in personal development and growth as a Senior Coach and Program Leader. He has worked with, been mentored and coached by some of the most progressive, transformational coaches in the industry.

With more than 13,000 hours of experience, he has coached almost one thousand people all over Europe and the States, including multimillionnaires, CEOs, actors and artists and is regarded by his peers as one of the most highly trained and experienced coaches in the world.

Ryan loves people and their lives, talking for hours, dogs, running up and down mountains, playing golf, recycling and being on time.

Contact: ryan@ryanmathie.com

Website: www.ryanmathie.com

LinkedIn: www.linkedin.com/in/ryanmathie

# Why *Purpose* Outweighs The Payday For Most Employees

## Dr Kylie Hutchings Mangion

As the *Millennial* generation slowly replaces the *Baby Boomer* generation, social scientists are seeing a change in how workers perceive their work.[1] Each generation brings a decidedly different perspective about the meaning of *work* and what it means to be a *worker,* and the attitude of those seniors is often both at odds with, and significantly more valuable than, that of their younger counterparts.

While salary levels, benefits, and added perks are always welcome, many of the globe's oldest employees arrive at work each day with a different type of compensation in mind: they want to accomplish a purpose through their daily effort. While yes, they still want to build their material wealth, they are also not willing to sell their integrity or self-worth to attain it. Instead, they are looking for meaning in what they do and why they do it, and statistics reveal that they are better workers than their younger colleagues because of the value of their more focused and purposeful attention.

If your company is looking for ways to improve its corporate metrics, you may be interested to learn about and potentially adopt the emerging *purpose-driven attitude* as your corporate cultural directive.

## Why Is *Purpose* Significant?

It is a natural aspect of humanity to want a purpose in life[2]. Most people aren't satisfied by attaining a goal for no other reason than to achieve it. Instead, they seek the sense of self-satisfaction, pride, and accomplishment that come with that success. That being said, the defining notion of *purpose* is a very personal one, and each individual will define and pursue their unique definition of purpose in a different way. However, as a group, those people who live and work with a sense of purpose are often more productive than those who don't embrace the purposeful lifestyle. Simply put: studies show that those people who rise every day with a sense of purpose can accomplish more, and be more productive overall, than those who don't have that outlook.

## The Value Of Purpose In A Corporate Setting From The Worker's Perspective

For employees, purposeful work is often the result of a dedicated search[3] for it both inside and outside their present employment. If they don't immediately understand the purpose of their daily labour, they will work to find it within the confines of their actual occupation or workplace. When they do discover a sense of meaning in their work, recent studies indicate that employees experience a series of benefits in the office and at home:

- Their productivity level tends to be higher;
- Their incomes also tend to be higher, and
- They actually live longer.

According to Mark Smith, Professor of Human Resource Management at the Grenoble School of Management,[4] '[worker] engagement distinguishes *just-enough* contributions [apart] from those efforts that make a difference' when evaluating the relative levels of worker satisfaction.

Further, he notes, employees permitted to channel their energies to make their work more meaningful often end up aligning their effort with corporate values and goals. In short, workers want to have a purpose in their work and companies that facilitate that drive will have a happier, more productive workforce.

## From The Employer's Perspective

From an economic standpoint, companies that embrace a *purposeful* culture can save money and improve productivity, with relatively little added investment needed.

Those organisations that don't see the value of, or implement, a workplace purpose-driven culture often pay a high price for that lapse:

- If having no purpose feeds a culture of low employee morale, then companies that lose workers because of low worker morale are also costing themselves significant resources. In fact, most organisations aren't aware of the expenses they incur because of low employee morale, which is often the cause of high worker turnover. That turnover cost is often much higher than corporate leadership realises.[5]
  In one study, the cost of replacing an upper management employee was estimated at over 200% of their annual salary, while the cost of replacing workers in the $30k - $75k range equaled at least 20% of their annual wage. Those costs include not just the expense incurred in generating the search criteria and conducting the hiring process, but also the costs generated through the on-boarding and training functions as well as the lost productivity of the worker, the impacted department, and the HR office during the transition.

If, instead, the company invested in improving its worker morale and enterprise culture, it could save those costs by reducing turnover and maintaining higher retention rates while gaining a more productive workforce at the same time.

- Employers who *talk the purpose talk* without implementing the philosophy in practice also pay a price. In another study,[6] 42% of surveyed UK workers reported that their employers did not act in conformance with the company's stated purpose and values, while 53% reported that corporate advertising was false on that issue. Workers who sense that management is not on board with the purpose-driven philosophy lose motivation, distrust their bosses, and reduce their productivity.

- Customers can also sense when there's a disconnect between what a company says and what they perceive the company is doing. When consumers suspect less-than-honourable activities on the part of a potential vendor, they will choose to shop elsewhere. Customers who actively experience the disconnect firsthand, through poor customer service, perhaps, will not only stop shopping there but may also post their negative impression online, where it can do immense harm to the corporate reputation. In fact, the aforementioned study concluded that not living up to the corporate assertion of purpose can do more damage to the company than not having the purposeful philosophy at all.

Overall, the research indicates that companies will do better economically and culturally when:

- They embrace a sense of purpose in their values and goals;
- Mandate its exercise at all levels of the corporate structure, and
- Encourage their employees to pursue their personal sense of purpose in all their daily efforts.

# How Leaders Can Establish and Maintain a Culture of Purpose?

## It Begins with You

Before we explore further how leadership can impact the purposeful activities of its workforce, stop to think about the personal level of purpose you bring to your leadership position: are you in this position because you need the job (for personal, financial, or other reasons)? Or because you want to be here and find joy in your work every day? How you answer that query will say a lot about how you run your organisation.

Our research shows that leaders who bring a sense of purpose to their own effort[7] will have a workforce that follows suit. For example, Australia's number one employer, *KPMG*, created a dedicated project - *The Purpose Initiative*[8] - to develop a higher sense of purpose in its workforce.

- The project began with a video that showed the company's contributions to historic events, including its execution of America's US$60 billion Lend-Lease Act[9] in support of the Allies during the Second World War.

- Employees were then encouraged to tell their stories about how their work at the company contributed to the betterment of the world.

- While company leaders hoped to get 10,000 stories by their November 2014, deadline, instead, they received over 42,000 responses by that date. But that wasn't the only overwhelming response:

- 90% of *KPMG* workers surveyed said that the Initiative increased their pride in their company, and

- The enterprise jumped 17 positions (from #80 to #63) up *Fortune Magazine's 2015 Best Companies to Work For*[10] list. (It reached #29 in 2017.)

*KPMG* is just one example of how financial compensation is often not the primary reason why workers remain with a valued employer.

## Purpose Powers Retention Strategies

In fact, our metrics show that a sense of purpose is often the key to avoiding turnover costs by retaining employees. As a leader, you probably use a range of retention strategies to achieve a variety of purposes, none of which may be designed to help you understand what drives your people.

- You may offer traditional incentives[11] such as pay bonuses, paid time off, or even gifts or trips as encouragement for continued good work. And while these do provide extra value and offer obvious recognitions that are valued by workers, they are also external to the employee's personal experience with the company.

- Alternatively, like many other leaders, you may be stuck in a *performance* model of leadership, which measures worker *success* by the number of widgets they produce, and only offers extra accolades when those numbers are good. Again, tracking only data that is external to the worker's personal experience will not build for you the workforce you want.

I suspect, then, that you are interested in creating a truly engaged and enlightened staff for your enterprise and are seeking both reasons and methods for pursuing that goal. That, in itself, is the sign of a good leader, so good for you.

## Begin by Assessing Their Current Realities

Most people have to work to support their lives, although some are fortunate to work because they want to, not because they have to. Your goal is to ensure that every worker is fulfilled by their work, regardless of their need. By doing so, you help them achieve their goals while also achieving the most beneficial outcome for your enterprise at the same time.

## Identify Their Motivations

While every worker is different and brings a different drive to the office each day, most are motivated by similar reasons to do well once they get there:

### Intrinsic motivations

Many workers bring their best work to everything they do simply because it's in their nature to do so. While it may be challenging to improve their activities, it will always be worthwhile to acknowledge the value that you have for the consistent value they bring.

### Personal investment in corporate goals

Your enterprise may focus on social goals that your employees embrace as a matter of personal preference. You may be gaining a higher level of performance because they see the organisation's success as their own.

### Satisfying individual projects

Even if the overall entity isn't totally on track with their personal drives, your company will still benefit if your workers are attending to individual projects that give them a reason to be especially highly engaged.

### An embracing team

Sometimes it's the people with whom they work that motivates the best performance of an employee. In many cases, the collective brain is more creative and productive than a single mind; you may be experiencing exceptional work from workers who are inspired by their colleagues.

### A sense of belonging

Sometimes, regardless of the work performed, employees engage well with the enterprise because they feel their effort matters to the success of its workforce. Simple tasks that are easily completed can add emotional value when they help a coworker to achieve a better result or redirect an issue to a more appropriate department.

Whatever it is that drives your individual workers, your business will benefit if you, as their leader, identify what it is that motivates them forward, then modify your leadership strategies to support them in those ways.

### Identify Your Strategy

Once you've recognised how your employees approach their work, your next task is to strategise how you are going to maximise those realities. A comprehensive strategy will encompass basic human-centred elements, regardless of the specifics of the work you want them to perform.

### Explain Why the Work is Being Done

Most employees will focus more attention and intention when they understand the value of the task they are performing. Connecting their activity to a greater value, a higher outcome, or a specific result gives them the opportunity to personally *buy into* the process as a whole. Workers who don't see the value in their activities, or who can't connect the exercise to a more significant purpose aren't likely to invest significant personal resources into its accomplishment. Leaders who don't distinguish the difference between the two are also not likely to see performance improvements in the latter group.

## Explain the Ultimate Value of their Labor

For most companies, each separate element of production is geared to create a specific product or service that, as an aggregate, is bigger and better than the sum of those parts. Workers who see the value in the finished product are more likely to produce a higher quality work effort to their particular aspect of it, as well as derive significant pride from the high quality of product once it's complete.

The *KPMG* story is an excellent example of this concept; when the workforce as a whole translated the work of the company to the better good of the community, their effort improved, and, with it, so did the standing of the company. You can use the story-telling technique employed by *KPMG* to find out how your staff feels about both their particular job and about your company in general. Ask each of your workers to write a rationale for how their personal effort feeds your corporate whole. The responses you receive will reveal the extent to which they feel a sense of purpose in their work - or not.

With that information available, you can begin to develop your strategy to add purpose to your corporate culture (if it's not there already), so you can enhance the life and work of your employees, as well as enhance the overall success of your company.

## Conclusion

The world's workforce is changing, and newer employees don't bring the same sense of dedication and purpose as the generation of workers they are replacing.

However, the evidence is clear that employees who bring a sense of purpose to their work will perform better and with higher results than those who don't. Leaders who adopt and practice a purposeful methodology set an example for their workers to follow.

Companies that embrace a purposeful culture and structure their activities to enhance their worker's sense of purpose will also enjoy a rise in their fortunes and reputations.

So what's your next step?

# References

[1] Vesty, L. (2016, September 16). *Millennials want purpose over paychecks. So why can't we find it at work?* Retrieved April 05, 2018, from https://www.theguardian.com/sustainable-business/2016/sep/14/millennials-work-purpose-linkedin-survey

[2] Taylor, S., PhD. (2013, July 13). *The Power of Purpose.* Retrieved April 05, 2018, from https://www.psychologytoday.com/us/blog/out-the-darkness/201307/the-power-purpose

[3] Gaskell, A. (2017, October 17). *The Modern Hunt For Purpose.* Retrieved April 05, 2018, from https://www.forbes.com/sites/adigaskell/2017/10/24/the-modern-hunt-for-purpose/#75401c9fcdd2

[4] (n.d.). Retrieved April 09, 2018, from https://en.grenoble-em.com/annuaire/mark-smith

[5] Boushey, H., & Glynn, S. J. (2012, November 12). *There Are Significant Business Costs to Replacing Employees.* Retrieved April 05, 2018, from https://www.americanprogress.org/wp-content/uploads/2012/11/CostofTurnover.pdf

[6] Warin, R. (2018, February 14). *Comment: Why purpose matters and four steps companies can take to get it right.* Retrieved April 5, 2018, from http://www.ethicalcorp.com/comment-why-purpose-matters-and-four-steps-companies-can-take-get-it-right

[7] ArcTree, B. (n.d.). *Seven things employees really want from Australia's top employers.* Retrieved April 5, 2018, from http://arctree.com.au/what-employees-really-want/

[8] Hannan, E. (2016, May 6). *How KPMG gave 6000 employees a higher purpose.* Read more: Http://www.afr.com/brand/boss/how-kpmg-gave-6000-employees-a-higher-purpose-20160427-gog7sa#ix-zz5CCEVnFMj Follow us: @FinancialReview on Twitter | financialreview on Facebook. Retrieved April 5, 2018, from http://www.afr.com/brand/boss/how-kpmg-gave-6000-employees-a-higher-purpose-20160427-gog7sa

[9] KPMG. (n.d.). History. Retrieved April 5, 2018, from https://home. kpmg.com/pk/en/home/about/overview/history.html

[10] Forbes. (2015). *100 Best Companies to Work For.* Retrieved April 5, 2018, from http://fortune.com/best-companies/2015/kpmg-63/

[11] Tullman, G. (2013, December 23). *Traditional Cash Bonuses Don't Really Work -- Try One of These 5 Instead.* Retrieved April 5, 2018, from https://www.forbes.com/sites/glentullman/2013/12/23/ traditional-cash-bonuses-dont-really-work-try-one-of-these-5-instead/#4c1051d03db3

## About Dr Kylie Hutchings Mangion

Dr Kylie Hutchings Mangion is a Cognitive Ergonomist and the Executive Director of Human CKOde.

As an expert in human cognitive performance, she specialises in human-centred leadership. Her flagship executive mentorship program helps Human Resource Leaders master the Art of Employee Retention.

She has over 25 years' experience in learning and development and the concept of instructional design and development under sound leadership management is at the core of her passion of how humans construct knowledge.

Dr Hutchings Mangion is also an Academic for Charles Sturt University and lectures across all faculties and within the Schools of Information Studies, Education, Graduate Policing and Biomedical Sciences, sharing with both faculty and students her extensive knowledge in the areas of cognitive processing, communications and human-centred practices. In the commercial setting, psychosocial and cognitive ergonomic principles from a human factors perspective form the basis of her focus, and she provides industry leaders with the necessary insights to optimise the human experience within their organisation's areas of leadership, design, capacity and performance.

Dr Kylie Hutchings Mangion  CAHRI EdD MEdTech BLDes (USQ)
BTeach (PAVE) (CQU)  Human CKODE

www.humanckode.com.au

kylie@humanckode.com.au

https://www.linkedin.com/in/dr-kylie-hutching-mangion

## Social/Relationships

Quality of life, quality of experience,
quality of environment, connection to family,
friends, community, work, social,
relationships, stress

# Am I Safe, Do I Belong, Do I Matter?

## Lesley Foley

It's been said many times that people are your most important asset.

They can also be a liability.

Depending on how they feel about their work, your people can be enthusiastic allies wholeheartedly invested in the success of the organisation, or disengaged clock-watchers barely even fulfilling their job functions.

Both are ambassadors for your brand.

Every leader's wish list includes a motivated, high performing team that goes above and beyond to create world class customer experiences. They want talented people who are dedicated to the vision and rave about working for the company.

But the reality is, leaders are more often frustrated about communication problems, low effort, low engagement, absenteeism, and conflict in their teams.

In 2013, a Gallup survey found that 87% of employees worldwide are not engaged at work. This means people are uninspired about their jobs and unfulfilled at work. Their energy levels are low, they find it hard to stay focused on their tasks and they don't really care much about the success of the business.

Furthermore, when good people leave these organisations, it has an unsettling effect on those left behind – they begin to question whether they should also move on, triggering a cycle of pessimism. Customers experience the uncertainty and negativity and the company reputation plummets.

So how can you turn this around?

Many employers believe they are already doing enough by giving their employees a fair salary, good working conditions and opportunities for promotion. But while these are good provisions, they are not enough to get the full attention and discretionary effort of your people.

> *"We have seen that unlocking discretionary effort can lead to a 20% uptick in productivity."*
>
> *Bev Messinger, CEO,*
> *Institution of Occupational Safety and Health.*

Employers are still unaware of the real needs of their employees - those rarely talked of, but fundamental human needs to feel safe, that you belong and that you matter.

These primary human needs run deep with people. A throw-back to times when our survival depended upon being part of a tribe, we still instinctively scan our environments today to see if these needs are being met or not.

We continually assess situations and relationships, noticing how we're being treated, whether we're liked and included, when we're ignored or disrespected, even unconsciously tuning into other people's tone of voice and body language to pick up the signals. It causes us an enormous amount of subconscious tension when we don't get these needs met. Many people experience this as low-level anxiety, stress and depression.

On the contrary, in any situation where we feel that we are safe, we belong and we matter, we naturally feel good. The experience of being safe, supported and valued by others gives us energy and confidence, and increases our sense of self-worth.

In the workplace, when people feel safe, they're calmer and more confident which helps them focus, think clearly and work with creativity and innovation. When they feel that they belong, there's a sense of everyone in this together, being part of a tribe. They'll take responsibility for, and pride in, the success of the organisation. When they feel they matter, they care right back - for the people they work with and for the business objectives. They work harder and are willing to develop themselves to give even more value.

Employees feel happy and motivated when these key needs are met, and they become more conscientious about the vision and goals of the organisation.

In other words, they become your collaborators in success.

*"Train people well enough so they can leave, treat them well enough so they don't want to."*

*Richard Branson.*

In my twenties, I worked in a secure accommodation unit for young people aged 12-16. The young people had been placed there for their own safety or for the safety of others. A *Secure Order* isn't given lightly to a child so their behaviour really had to involve serious risk before they'd be given a place. Their qualifying behaviours included: theft, robbery, joy-riding in stolen cars, alcohol and substance abuse, violent crimes, dangerous activities and promiscuity.

Typically, their childhood histories would include poverty, neglect and/or abuse. Growing up in struggling, dysfunctional homes, they rarely felt safe, that they belonged or that they mattered much to the adults around them.

Life is very stressful when your deep-seated human needs aren't met, and these youngsters played out their distress in the most dangerous of ways. Often they'd find safety and a sense of belonging in small gangs of like minded individuals, whilst stealing cars or committing serious crimes gave them an experience of feeling significant, even powerful, if only for a short while. Their outrageous behaviour was often like a test to see if they mattered to anyone at all, and sadly, suicide attempts were all too common.

I'm sure not one of them ever wanted to be caught and sent off to live in secure accommodation, but a strange thing often happened when they did.

Living in units of up to eight young people, they soon got to know the others living there, as well as the ten care workers assigned to their unit. Their days were structured with three healthy meals, school lessons in micro-classes, scheduled breaks, and evening activities, such as swimming, badminton, football, and table tennis. And every evening, at 9.45pm, each would retire to their own comfortable, secure room where the door would be locked all night unless they needed anything from the night staff.

Each young person had a designated care worker for the duration of their stay, and they benefitted from access to professionals they may not have seen for years, for example, doctor, dentist, optician or educational psychologist.

Over time, the predictable routine coupled with consistent emotional and physical care helped them to move from *survive* to *thrive*. There were no miracle cures for the neglect and trauma they'd suffered but it was remarkable to see the difference that could be made by simply meeting their most fundamental human needs to be safe, to have a sense of belonging, and to feel that they mattered.

It was most poignant when it came time to leave. Most would have mixed feelings – excitement and trepidation - about going back to live in their communities, so in the build up to their leaving date they'd have day visits and overnight stays back home to help them with the transition. Often, all would go well until the last weekend, and then they'd fall back into some risky behaviour that would earn them a continuation of their *Secure Order* for another three months. Whether consciously done or not, many of these youngsters just didn't want to leave.

At a primal level, humans need to feel safe, that they belong and they matter, it's part of our instinctive survival mechanism and we'll go to extraordinary lengths to get these met, even if it means losing our freedom.

In a business environment, people may be less vulnerable but the unconscious drive is the same. Leaders who genuinely pay attention to meeting these needs stand to gain the deep loyalty and trust of their people, as well as the satisfaction of building a really great place to work.

The most amazing thing is, all this is achieved through relationships. Here are some specific things you can do to help meet these needs:

### Safe

Develop a no-blame culture where people feel safe to talk about problems and mistakes. Build trust by staying calm when things go wrong and managing emotional reactions, particularly anger. Rather than blowing up, take some time to cool off, get some perspective and think before you act so no-one feels attacked or unduly criticised.

### Belong

Invite and include others' opinions and ideas, especially from the quieter people on your team. Unite your tribe together by having two-way conversations about the company vision and values. Develop rituals that everyone can be part of to increase the sense of identity and connection.

## Matter

Communicate well with your people, listen empathically, and always treat them with respect and dignity. Be transparent with important information and keep them updated with changes. Acknowledge their efforts and appreciate them. Often.

Leadership can be lonely. This is especially true if you're the only person with their heart in the business. The truth is, you can't do it alone, you need others to pull with you.

When you see the human in every employee and give them what they fundamentally need - not just to survive, but to really thrive - you unlock a treasure trove of resources and value for your business.

If you make it top priority to take care of your people, they'll take care of your business.

And you'll soon find that you feel safe, that you belong and you matter more, too.

## References

- Bev Messinger, (2018). Institute of Directors (IoD) roundtable discussion.
- Richard Branson (2014).

## About Lesley Foley

Lesley Foley is an Emotional Intelligence coach and trainer who specialises in transforming organisations by transforming relationships.

Her work focuses on helping people understand themselves and others in both their professional and personal lives to create new possibilities for connection and collaboration.

Trained in *The Enneagram in Business* (personality profiling), Nonviolent Communication, Neuro-Linguistic Programming, and Emotional Freedom Technique/Matrix Reimprinting.

Lesley also draws from experience working in education, engineering and oil industry corporations and from an intensive, crazy journey of home educating her three children.

In a nutshell, her work is about self-acceptance, self-mastery, compassion and transformation.

www.eq2lead.uk

lesley@eq2lead.uk

https://www.linkedin.com/in/lesley-foley-eq2lead/

# It's Not Networking – It's Marketing!

## Sandi Goddard

Why network? Primarily to build connections and to promote a business, products, services or perhaps yourself.

Some claim they never network. Drill down and you may find they belong to a *Rotary Club* or *Round Table*, a trade association or a golf club.

I believe humans have always networked. At ancient gatherings, goods and skills were bartered or traded; ties were developed and strengthened by marrying daughters or sisters to scions of the wealthy or powerful. Those events were hotbeds of communication. Innovation spread, virus-like, across countries and continents.

The Black Death decimated populations and impoverished the Church, but it raised per-capita incomes, and expanded consumption and commerce.

Guilds replaced extended families binding individuals closely, particularly in times of crisis, discouraging individualism and encouraging collective institutions.

By the 17th century, coffee houses, described as *seats of English liberty*, became the centres of communication. Great social levellers associated with equality, republicanism, politics and business.

People communicating through blood ties, commerce, industry, mutual interests and with a show of goods: *networking!*

Twenty years ago, I and three of my team joined *Business Network International (BNI)*, newly launched in London, and my business prospered. Since then there has been an explosion in networking groups and events, providing a means to a job, promotion, and a valuable source of contacts.

Laura Hurran, founder and executive director of *BNI Central London* and co-national director Italy, believes you cannot ignore networking and posts 21 year plus memberships as proof that networking delivers. Her tips include: give to gain; don't expect business immediately; honour the event; use *LinkedIn* not only to keep in touch but as your contact system.

Matthew Crummack, CEO of *Go Compare*, will no doubt concur, his database goes back to his University days. Because: you never know when you may need to call on someone.

Some business leaders see networking as irrelevant to their growth. For others it is a fundamental marketing tool. They take a strategic approach – there is NO SUBSTITUTE FOR PERSONAL CONTACT. They track all contacts, follow ups and results, run their own events and, often, build their own national and international associations.

Professor Ros Taylor, internationally acclaimed clinical psychologist, CEO of *Ros Taylor Company*, author of eight books on confidence and leadership, and one of the UK's top executive coaches, outlines the psychology of networking as: great networkers are passionately interested in meeting new people. They are good listeners; look for opportunities to help; make connections and build relationships.

Are people born with the ability to network – without a doubt. But for those who are not naturally *smiley,* business coach, Erkan Ali recommends investing in oneself, developing the soft skills we might lack. Learn how to engage, hire a voice coach, practice ice breakers and make wall flowers into bosom buddies. And as with everything – there must be commitment.

## Your Networking Objective

How many events have we attended, packed with strangers. If we are lucky there is a guest list, which we scan hoping to recognise someone. Then, list in one hand and glass in the other, we start to *mingle!*

Why do it? Define your business objectives. And your audience. Jane Michell, CEO and founder of diet delivery service, *janeplan.com* uses networking to build her multi-million pound business. She is passionate about her business; resolute and focused about networking. She attends as many events and groups as possible, often going to breakfast, lunch and evening meetings on the same day.

## Attitude

Networking is a communications dance. Acting coach and retail business development expert, James Newall offers these observations: be open to opportunities, enjoy the occasion, try five or six until you find networks that suit you. Greet people with a smile and a strong, confident handshake. And don't forget – when you are talking to someone, keep eye contact. Or as communications expert, author and speaker, Kay White says to make an impact we need to *show up and sparkle.*

## Choosing your Network

According to the *Theory of Social Identity*, our sense of self is informed partly by the group to which we belong. The 551 London coffeehouses of 1771, each with a specific clientele recognised by occupation or attitude, were eventually replaced by *Chambers of Commerce*, while gentlemen's clubs drew the more aristocratic clientele. Any man claiming to be a *gentleman* belonged to a club closely corresponding with the trade or social/political identity he felt most defined him.

## Do your research

Do you want single gender, formal or informal, trade related, virtual or face-to-face? Or both? What time of day suits you best? Try out a wide range to find the best events for you. Tanya Mann Rennick, founder of networking organisation *The Oyster Club*, describes the three pillars of a great network as information, education and support. And attending different events means you may meet that one person who will change your life. Check out networking events for Continuing Professional Development, research value … and enjoyment.

Some useful tips, if you are new to networking or in an unfamiliar situation. Look for people standing alone or for *open* groups, where you can easily engage in conversation.

Prepare and practice opening gambits. Questions are generally the most effective. People usually like to talk about themselves, so show interest in your fellow networkers. Or you could simply walk over to the bar and wait for people to come to you, like British fashion designer and 60s icon, Zandra Rhodes, who stands out with her strong personal style.

## The Elevator Pitch

Three words that turn grown men and women to mindless jelly! Ideally it is a memorable, concise and effective definition of your business, product or service, including your value proposition, delivered in less than two minutes.

Practice your *Elevator Pitch*. It is perfect for formal networks, where you may have up to 60 seconds to introduce yourself.

In an informal setting, you need something shorter. Hone, or pay someone to write, pithy narratives that are memorable and that you can call on depending on the occasion. Think of it as your *war chest* and don't forget – passion is key!

## Working a room requires time management.

Avoid spending all evening with one or two people, unless of course this is your objective. Ten minutes, or so, is ideal. Develop techniques for moving on. Facilitating introductions is an effective tool, allowing you to take one person over to another, leaving you free to move on.

Take your own, highly legible, badge. Those supplied at networks may be too small. You simply need your name and company, or perhaps your role (environmentalist/management consultant/architect). Take some brochures or direct mail pieces to give out, in case you are asked for more information.

## Dressing the Part, Protocol and Dress Codes

If there is pre-event networking, use it to your advantage. Your preferred contacts may arrive early and leave promptly. Equally, the end of an event can be the perfect time for developing acquaintances. Attendees often stay back to talk to the speaker or catch up with latecomers.

While the whole point of networking is to make connections, one must maintain good manners. Talking over your host or a guest speaker – or forgetting to thank them when you leave, is not endearing.

Some networks may have a dress code, so it's worth checking ahead. Dress appropriately for the occasion and your business sector – inappropriate or scruffy appearance undermines credibility.

Or in the words of Coco Chanel: "Dress shabbily and they remember the dress; dress impeccably and they remember the woman." (or the man!)

## Follow up

You may or may not want to give out cards, but you do need to collect contact information. How will you process it?

Take notes on the back of the card you have just been given. It is surprising how little information there is on business cards. A week after meeting someone it may be difficult to work out what they do and why you wanted to keep in touch.

Smart phones help. You can scan cards or badges, make notes and transfer information to your CRM system.

What is your follow up plan – email, phone, social media? Nigel Botterill, CEO and founder of *Entrepreneurs Circle* takes the long view. He uses *InfusionSoft* to manage his contacts which he keeps until they *buy or die!*

## Keep in touch

Implement helpful, informative follow up strategies that develop your relationships. And if you promise to connect, send information or meet for coffee, don't forget. It only takes one small thing to undermine that first, good, impression.

## Return on Investment

You will be spending time, money and adrenaline – so review your return on investment annually. Have you achieved your original objectives? Do they need refining? Are you making useful contacts? Is there long-term gain? Will you be able to develop strong relationships? Are these the right networks for you?

# Top Tips

- Identify Objectives
- Research and Select
- Passion and Focus
- Look the part
- Icebreakers and wall flowers
- Work the room
- Connect and engage
- Listen attentively
- Be present
- Develop relationships
- Exit gracefully
- Follow up enthusiastically

## About Sandi Goddard

A strategic brand and management consultant, Sandi Goddard has been a prolific networker for over 20 years. Using her extensive database, she launched her own business networking lunches in 2004, facilitating relationship building between business women. In 2014 she began her business leaders'  interviews to understand their views on networking. Some of which are included in this article.

Sandi works with business leaders, boards and leadership teams, using the experience informed by her corporate background with global enterprises to prepare and enable clients to achieve demonstrably significant growth and profitable, £multi-million returns. And has helped SMEs in finance, technology and industry to achieve £multi-million exit.

She understands the demands facing business leaders from time and budget constraints, developing client facing strategies and ensuring profitability to recruiting and managing great teams.

Her approach, and very personal service delivery, is results-driven. Sandi aims for strategic alignment and congruence between business objectives and ethos; promoting enterprises and individuals to the widest possible audiences; building brand value; delivering positive bottom-line impact and increased market share.

Her clients look for more than strategic marketing and business consulting; they want a trusted advisor, a sounding board or a Non-Executive Director.

http://www.goddard-delaney.mobi

http://www.goddard-delaney.com

Skype: sandij.goddard

Twitter @sandigoddard

LinkedIn https://www.linkedin.com/in/sandigoddard/

Face Book https://www.facebook.com/sandi.goddard.5

Instagram https://www.instagram.com/goddardsandi/

# Best Practice

Performance, productivity, efficacy, effectiveness, efficiency, fast-tracking, current best thinking, compliance, governance, due diligence

# Real Leaders Do Not Look @ The Numbers

## Amanda Fisher

One of the scariest things you will ever hear is when someone says, *"Let's just look at the numbers."* You see, it's not about looking *at* the numbers; it's about looking *through* the numbers to the stories they tell.

Leaders who look at the numbers are usually only looking at the historical perspective. When the numbers aren't what they expect them to be, their instinctive thought is how to improve the bottom line result.

Immediate actions are often to slash costs, cut staff or cull any extra costs that aren't deemed necessary to making sales or increasing revenue. Alternatively, they berate the sales team for a poor effort in not meeting their sales targets. Neither option is good for the team or the business in the long run.

Financial reports by definition are reporting past history. Hopefully those reports are produced in a timely manner so necessary decisions can be made quickly to redress issues and challenges that may have arisen and arrest the negative turn of events so as not to exacerbate the issues.

Equally when the financial reports are showing better than expected progress, this isn't an automatic signal to reduce the focus on the numbers or spend money on a business luxury that isn't integral to the vision and direction of the business.

Improved results may be temporary (a one-off project) or permanent (ongoing increased revenue), either way, continued focus on the numbers ensures the improved position is maintained or built upon.

Leaders who look at the numbers usually risk making knee jerk decisions that are shallow and reactionary and short term. Such decisions are the result of seeing numbers as flat and only two-dimensional.

There is, of course, a time and place for simply flat numbers, for reviewing history and taking it at face value. Statutory financial reports are used for determining tax liabilities, whereas it is in the management reports where the true value lies for real leaders.

Why is it then, that different people see the numbers differently, and even two accountants looking at the same figures may have a different take on what they mean? Some will see a problem to fix; others will see a future to chase.

It's the difference between looking *at* the numbers and looking *through* the numbers.

Real leaders are able to:

1. Read the numbers, then
2. Interpret the numbers, then
3. Apply their insights to the numbers and then
4. Make decisions and take action.

Leaders who just read the numbers are essentially simply looking *at* the numbers. Leaders who interpret the numbers and then apply their insights are looking *through* the numbers. It's these extra layers of consideration, contemplation and then connection that make real leaders stand out from the crowd.

The application of insight is in the approach taken to reviewing the numbers.

Regardless of my many years' of experience reviewing numbers, I still have a checklist of questions I ask myself when I'm reviewing them, just like the airplane pilot with his pre take-off checklist.

The approach I take is by:

1. Applying my wisdom. What are the known facts, data or knowledge I have about the business? What are the recent challenges and successes within the business?

2. Applying general knowledge. What is the current state of the economy that has impacted the business? What changes are likely in the future?

3. Considering the past. What past experiences and learnings can I bring to the way I view these numbers while at the same time being emotionally disconnected from the outcome?

4. Bringing a deliberate curiosity and questioning mind. What questions can I ask about these numbers? What are they telling me?

5. Being prepared to go down a rabbit hole to see whether it brings a different perspective to the numbers and what they mean.

6. Asking what numbers stand out as being odd, out of place or different?

7. Applying a future vision lens to the numbers. How can they help determine and define the future of the business? Are they in alignment with the stated vision and mission of the business?

8. And lastly, I deliberately leave room to question the unknown. What are we missing? What else is there we need to be thinking about?

The approach and attitude you choose to bring to the numbers can make a significant difference to the decision making process. It's about taking a bright, positive future approach. Looking through the numbers allows you to create the future not just replicate the past with a slight tweak to it.

The reason why different people interpret the numbers differently and have different insights is often in large part due to their personal history, past experiences and either limited by or enhanced by their capacity to deliberately apply their insights and expressed wisdom.

Those who share their insights and wisdom see a different future from those who see only history and a problem to fix. The latter are just looking *at* the numbers, not *through* the numbers.

Looking through the numbers is refusing to see them at face value. Only by applying insights and interpretations might you see the foundations of a better future.

This is the approach that makes the numbers jump out, become three-dimensional as it were, as they integrate with the actual operations of the business, its people, projects, systems and processes. All are inter-related and must be considered in conjunction with each other. Focusing on any one area of business in isolation is a recipe for a modern business disaster.

When the numbers aren't stacking up the way they are expected to, there's always a reason why. The key is to be able to pinpoint the area of weakness as quickly as possible by looking through the numbers. Whether it's poor staff morale, out-dated or legacy systems and processes, new staff who aren't up to speed yet, products or services that no longer meet the customer or clients needs, customer or client churn rates, a sales team under performing; timely decisions can change the future.

Whilst looking through the numbers may pinpoint the problem area, a strong effective leader can delve further into why that is the case.

Simplistic surface answers are rarely the right ones.

Invariably there's a deeper reason why processes go off the rails and that's usually when it's time to explore that rabbit hole and find out what the issue really is.

Consider this example of a real life, *Flat Number Tragedy.*

The business is a large agricultural operation owned by overseas investors with a key manager ('John') overseeing the operations and the investors' main point of contact ('Bob').

John is an insightful leader who interprets the numbers, provides insights and asks smart questions of the accounting team. One of his roles is to provide a detailed quarterly report to the investors. Here he brings his wealth of knowledge and expertise, his detailed knowledge of the day-to-day operations, insights from weekly management meetings, his understanding of the economy, commodity prices, currency fluctuations and his vision for the future.

Should one of the operational managers make a poor decision or if economic circumstances change suddenly, he's immediately able to take action to minimise any downside.

The quarterly report had been provided with extensive detail and insights from John. Bob had a string of questions, all flat number questions. For example, why is the valuation of the properties not the same as the reports provided by the valuer? What is this number made up of? Why has this number decreased from last year? And the list went on.

Bob has never seen the business operations and it's fair to say he's a traditional accountant just looking *at* the numbers. His questions suggest he hasn't used his ability to interpret or apply insights to what he was provided. It may be he sees his role as a check and balance one, not needing to take time to more fully understand the business, its various commercial moving parts and how they interact in a three-dimensional space to produce the numbers that tell the story.

Bob's report to the investors is a factual summary of the

numbers, the business value and their return on investment (ROI).

Decisions are made based on those numbers. John is required to develop detailed feasibility analyses for any opportunities that arise and present these to the investors knowing that they are only interested in business value and ROI.

Great opportunities are left on the table due to the investors looking *at* the numbers approach.

Real leaders look *through* the numbers, not *at* them, seeing the numbers as three-dimensional and integrated within the business operations.

They apply insights and interpretation skills and use the numbers as a leadership tool to help identify the weakest link in the business, understand why that's the case and then seek to find a solution to the root of the problem, not being distracted by the obvious surface answer.

When leading a business, be the leader who looks *through* the numbers.

## About Amanda Fisher

Amanda Fisher is a Chartered Accountant who is passionate about helping business owners understand their numbers.

Having worked principally with small to medium-sized business owners for over 30 years, Amanda understands first-hand the challenges and stresses of running a business.

Amanda spent her post-university years in CFO roles in a range of industries and has also owned several successful accounting practices.

In 2015, Amanda realised her passion lay in helping business owners to better understand their numbers to provide improved cash flow and better business outcomes.

Amanda brings a unique blend of business intrigue, a deep understanding of the numbers and the ability to simplify the complex.

Amanda has written three books - *Unscramble Your Numbers, The Connected Accounting Practice* and the Amazon number 1 bestseller, *Connected Technology*. She is also the creator of the *Business Cash Flow Mastery Program*, the *Xero Optimisation Workshop;* and is an in-demand public speaker

Amanda is a Fellow of the *Institute of Chartered Accountants* in Australia and graduated with Merit from the University of New South Wales.

https://amandafisher.com.au

LinkedIn: https://www.linkedin.com/in/amandafisherca/

# What Business Can Learn From The Military On Leadership

## Mike Davis-Marks OBE

In a recent survey, 72% of respondents cited their boss as the main reason for changing jobs. In separate research, over 75% of employees questioned said that they were disengaged with their work and were doing it for the money rather than any higher purpose. These statistics are just the tip of the iceberg; despite modern advances and labour saving automation, employee engagement in the UK is poor at best.

Separately, many business leaders don't know the difference between good management and good leadership, thinking that a well run organisation is the same as a well-led organisation.

It isn't.

A well managed organisation is all about processes and procedures. A well-led organisation is one where the people who work there know what the company stands for and their part in it, are engaged in shaping the processes and procedures and feel valued for what they do. They are treated as individuals and are fully engaged in what they do and not just a number on the finance department's spreadsheet.

The thing is, a company with a great leadership culture (rather than just well run) fares better than one that has a poor leadership culture. In general, in these companies, productivity tends to be higher, staff absenteeism (pulling a sickie) and staff turnover are lower, as are recruitment and training costs, all of which improves the bottom line significantly.

Better still, the workplace is a happy place in which to be and employees become natural advocates for the business they are in, leading to more effective marketing.

And the evidence supports this. Between 2008 and 2010, when the UK was in a deep recession, those companies who were judged to have a good leadership culture as defined above, averaged growth of 12% in that period, whilst companies that were judged to be poorly led, shrank by 32% - that's a massive 44% difference and just because of the way the company is led.

What's not to like?

## Lessons from the Military

Military leadership is often stereotyped (not helped by Hollywood) as either Colonel Blimp types, completely out of touch with the modern world, or by ruddy faced sergeants shouting orders on a drill parade. In my experience, based on 36 years in the Royal Navy, this couldn't be further from the truth. The same survey where an average of 72% of people cited their boss as the main reason for leaving the company, also showed some extremes.

At one end of the spectrum, a well-known FMCG company produced a statistic of 84% for leadership driven exits, whilst at the other end, an organisation of over 150,000 employees had only 2% of people leaving because of their boss. In case you hadn't guessed it, that second organisation was the UK Armed Forces, in which I was proud to have served.

Sure, about 14,000 men and women join and leave the Royal Navy, British Army and RAF every year, but that is for a variety of reasons - end of engagement or commission, separation, only intended to serve for 5 - 10 years, desire to settle down and raise a family, but poor leadership only figures in 2% of exit surveys.

So they must clearly be doing something right.

## Military Leadership - Four things to think about

Leadership training starts very early across most ranks in the UK Armed Forces (UKAF). People are seen as the most important asset and are developed as leaders from Day 1, irrespective of whether they join as Officers or other ranks/ratings. Indeed, approximately a third of all Officers come up through the ranks anyway, having been developed as a leader from the start of basic training.

In the world class training I received in my time in the Navy, including training to command a nuclear submarine, which I was lucky and privileged to do, the leadership aspects could be broken down into four key areas, which a leader needs to grasp if he or she is to be effective. Three of them follow, but not unreservedly, Adair's three circles of *Team, Task* and *Individual*. A fourth one, equally important, if not more so, is about leading oneself, doing the right thing and setting a good example.

Each of these will be taken in turn.

## Task

Every organisation has a mission (or should have). At the strategic level, this is often called a *Vision* and is communicated by a *Vision Statement*.

At the tactical level, this might be project aims and objectives or if you happen to be commanding a nuclear submarine, the mission.

Either way, everyone in the organisation should be really clear what the vision, project goals or mission objectives are. Everyone. Really Clear.

And that falls down to the leadership, whether it be the CEO/Board for the overall vision or project leaders and submarine captains for the tasks or missions.

Clarity of purpose - why are we here and what must we achieve is the compass needle in every organisation, pointing the direction to be taken and the *why* it is needed. As Simon Sinek says in *Start with Why*, *why* gives everyone an understanding of the purpose of the company, the need it is trying to meet and something to believe in. A good leader knows this and makes sure everyone in his or her circle is fully aware of it.

## Team

Ensuring that the team work effectively together, sharing information and supporting each other is one of the most important aspects of leadership.

Nowhere is this more important than on board a submarine, dived deep beneath the waves often for several months at a time, so my experience of the best teamwork has been honed in the most unique of circumstances.

Sadly, in everyday life, there is a tendency, even within teams, to work in silos and to retain information, under old fashioned models of chain of command hierarchies, where *information is power* and holding on to it rather than sharing is the norm. This leads to, *inter alia*, duplication of effort and a consequential waste of precious resources (time, money, creativity, thought etc) as well as a complete under utilisation of all the talent available within an organisation or team.

A good leader will ensure his or her team are pulling in the same direction (clarity of purpose) and working together well as a team, sharing information with each other and balancing the team dynamics so that team members strengths are utilised best and avoiding duplication of effort.

Collaboration, not knowledge is power and the leader that employs a collaborative approach, internally and externally is much more likely to succeed ultimately.

## Individual

Whilst a good leader is focussing on setting the vision clearly and ensuring the team is working effectively together, he or she also needs to consider the individual. Everyone is different, with unique strengths and weaknesses. Their motivations will be different too, as will personal circumstances. By far and away the most important quality a leader can have in this regard, is empathy. Empathy is vital, because it allows good leaders to consider the impact of decision making from another person's perspective, as well as address any specific concerns that individuals may have.

In a small team, this is completely possible, but for the CEO of a very large organisation, employing thousands of people, they can only apply it to those immediate around them - personal staff and the Board of Directors for example. The important aspect here is to lead from the front and require that the Directors apply the same principles to the next level down and so on. A good leader, however, will need to monitor the cascading culture from the bottom up, taking time to visit and talk to employees lower down in the organisation to see whether the message and the culture is percolating down as intended. The best leaders do this much of the time, so that the workforce feel their issues are being addressed.

## Setting a good example

Newspapers are full of Chief Executives and Directors being awarded eye watering salaries whilst lower paid workers being paid very moderate wages that haven't kept pace with inflation.

Leadership is also about setting the right example for the organisation - leading from the front. In Simon Sinek's book, *Leaders Eat Last*, he makes the point that in the military it is customary for ordinary soldiers, sailors, or marines to be fed before their officers, so that they know that the officers' responsibilities to support them first is being taken seriously. This creates a very strong bond between leader and led, so that when things are not going well, which they will at some point, then both parties know that they can depend on each other.

Good self awareness, or emotional intelligence, as Sean Foley makes a brilliant case for in *Fit For Purpose Leadership Book 1* is essential for a leader to gauge his or her impact on people and ensure they are connecting with them. Setting a good example - doing the right thing earns good leaders the respect they need to get the best out of people. By being a role model to their people, a good leader is showing them how to conduct themselves and creates the right environment for unlocking their potential through developing and supporting them.

### Conclusion

I believe that business has much to learn from the military with respect to leadership. The military instinctively understand the importance of people in producing and maintaining a world class capability. After all, a billion pound nuclear submarine is useless without the people to operate it effectively. Military leadership, at all levels, is very good at balancing the needs of the task, team and individuals, whilst setting a good example themselves, and is critical in ensuring that the best possible culture for inspiring and motivating people, developing them both as individuals and as part of a team, thereby achieving something money can't buy - ultimate job satisfaction and peak performances from the team.

After all, it's about people - it's always about people.

# References

- Sinek. S. (2011). *Start with Why.* Penguin
- Sinek. S. (2017). *Leaders Eat Last.* Portfolio Penguin
- Foley. S (2018). *Article in Fit for Purpose Leadership #1.* Writing Matters Publication
- Ref: John Adair's Action-Centred Leadership https://www. bl.uk/people/john-adair

## Mike Davis-Marks OBE

Mike Davis-Marks (MDM) enjoyed a 36 year career in the Royal Navy, having wanted to join the Service since the age of seven. During that time, he served in a wide variety of leadership roles in both submarines and surface ships, culminating in a testing three year command of the hunter killer nuclear powered submarine, *HMS Turbulent*.
He has also navigated a submarine to the North Pole (twice), taught Officer Cadets leadership at Britannia Royal Naval College, held a diplomatic post at the British Embassy in Washington DC (during the period of 9/11) and was awarded the OBE for his part in planning and running the International Fleet Review in 2005.

Since leaving the Navy in 2013, he joined an exciting group of Social Entrepreneurs called *Ethos,* who are looking at how technology and innovation can be used to drive collaborations into solving complex social and environmental problems and are also experimenting on the *Future of Work.* MDM qualified as a NLP practitioner in 2012 and believes that people are a company's most important asset and that investing in your workforce will deliver much greater dividends than merely trying to maximise shareholder profit.

www.ethosvo.org

LinkedIn: https://www.linkedin.com/in/mike-davis-marks-081b4212/

Twitter: @jollijacktar

# The Really Wild Leader

### Steven Shove, MBA, DipM

*"Life is a great adventure or nothing!"*

*Helen Keller*

Leadership is an adventure!

When planning an adventure to a new area of the globe I choose my expedition leaders and my team with a great deal of care and precision, for if I don't my clients and I may not come back. I seek the best and I seek those whom I trust – with my life!

This has led me to work with some of the most trusted and capable leaders in the world. It has been the same in my professional life as a business person, coach and educator too.

Like the weather - markets, regulations, technology, customer expectations and products for example, are always changing. Like vast areas of the rain forest - sales territories are frequently unexplored. Like expedition teams - the teams we come to rely upon are ever more varied, geographically dispersed, transactional or piecemeal in nature.

To survive and thrive in such conditions, we need a leader who can see us through such challenges and leverage the opportunities. I call these, *really wild leaders*.

So, what do they look like?

In the paragraphs below, I introduce ten characteristics that I deem to be some of the traits of a *really wild leader* - that is a leader whom you would trust to take you into the most challenging of environments, situations or circumstances, whom you would actively follow despite the odds.

Ten traits of a *really wild leader*:

1. Inspire and dare to venture
2. Set a clear direction and keep track of progress
3. Build trust
4. Be authentic
5. Communicate with excellence
6. Personally, connect and engage
7. Love people and the world about you
8. Serve and remain humble
9. Be resilient
10. Be consistent but willing to change

## 1. Inspire and dare to venture

*Really wild leaders* are not afraid to try new things or explore new lands. They recognise that staying put, whilst sometimes an essential short-term survival technique, is rarely a long-term strategy. Their minds are continually looking to new horizons and evaluating what might come next whilst protecting what is important now. They confidently inspire and rally their people and resources to act with a sense of purpose and urgency that can get even the most incredible things done.

Consider Elon Musk and his decision to make humans an interplanetary species. He determined that the existence of the human race is by no means guaranteed if we remain solely on our present celestial island. He developed this into a vision that motivated him and inspired others. He dared to risk his incredible personal wealth to challenge the status quo that rocket travel was too expensive and changed the nature of space travel forever. His staff follow him and his dream. They are not commanded to do so.

How do you inspire others? Why do they follow you? Where do you wish to take them?

## 2. Set a clear direction and keep a track of progress

When leading others in the mountains a mountain leader will be very precise in setting their goal and direction. They will also check and take regular bearings to know exactly where they are or use other navigational features to keep them on track. They will regularly appraise their teams of progress and let them know as accurately as they can what they can expect and when whilst on their journey. Their journey may not be straight, but they will always know where they are relative to their destination.

One of my colleagues, who was recently awarded an MBE by the Queen for his services to leadership development and survival training in the RAF, and who is also an *International Mountain Leader*, recently told me of an occasion when after hours and several kilometres of mountaineering he arrived just a few metres from his planned destination. I was really impressed until he stopped me in my tracks and told me that he had failed. He was on assessment in the fog. Had he arrived just a few metres in another direction he may have stepped over a precipice which would have led to certain death.

*Really wild leaders* set a clear direction and go to great lengths to make sure they and their entire team know where they are on their journey and what lies ahead. If you asked each member of your team where your organisation is going and what progress had been made, how similarly would they reply?

### 3. Build trust

For any leader to reach their full potential they must first be trusted. If not, their teams and the people they influence will never fully support them. Trust is earned by setting out your stall and honouring it, by being consistent with your behaviour, making the right choices and managing expectations.

As well as developing one's personal trust, a *really wild leader* will build and foster trust between each member of their team - internal, external, physically present and remote.

Perhaps the finest example of trust is the trust earned by Ernest Shackleton when his ship, the *Endurance* became trapped and sank in the Antarctic ice. His team trusted him to survive camping out on the floating ice for more than a year, to then embark on a highly dangerous journey in open boats to the remote and deserted Elephant Island and again when he ventured out on the most challenging nautical mission across the Antarctic Ocean in one of their remaining small boats on the promise that he would return to rescue them. They followed his instructions to the letter whilst he was away and true to his word, he returned with a rescue ship to find every single member of his team alive. *Really Wild Leadership* and mutual trust at its best! Imagine what you could achieve if you were trusted to such a degree!

Which behaviours might you further develop to increase your own trust or that across your organisation?

### 4. Be authentic

I was recently running a leadership programme for a number of government ministers, CEOs and other executives of banks and the subject was, *authentic leadership in a competitive world*.

In his wonderful book, *Discover Your True North*, Bill George recommended that leaders find their sweet spot and be true to themselves by creating working environments that enable them and their teams to operate according to the values and principles they hold dear.

Some of my clients explained that in reality this is not always easy, particularly when the environment in which you work is incredibly complex and the impact of your right choices might lead to outcomes for some that you would rather avoid. Doing the right thing can often be painful!

We concluded that a *really wild leader* will always do his or her best to live according to their principles and values, to change their working environment where and when they can on their path towards ever closer alignment. Where they definitely cannot make a difference, they will have the courage to move to a place in which they can.

Are you living and leading according to the principles and values you hold dear? If you feel light and unburdened by your choices, you probably are. If there is a nagging or knot in your stomach - what will you choose to change?

### 5. Communicate with excellence

During World War Two there was a poster that stated, *careless words cost lives!* I would add to this, *and actions too.*

Before allowing someone on expedition, I run an exercise to develop and assess each candidate's ability to communicate with clarity, empathy and encouragement. I also evaluate their behaviours throughout each selection process. If I don't and then allow them to join a trip to the Arctic for example, I run the risk that lives may be lost or clients not served well.

I have noted throughout my career that the more senior a person becomes the impact of their words reaches a point when it is amplified exponentially. What may have at one point been acceptable to share out loud, may in fact now result in consequences far beyond expectations.

For better or worse, a word from some people can change the entire performance of the global stock markets for instance. Consider Warren Buffet or various comments made by our friend Elon Musk! In just one tweet about taking his company *Tesla* private, Elon in August 2018 added 7% to the value of the company's stock. It rose so fast, that the SEC suspended trading and launched legal action against him for misleading the stock market.

If the power of a leader's words can be so strong, then what of their actions? When observing leaders at work, I notice that people are far more likely to model what someone does than what they say.

So how to communicate?

Like any indigenous peoples, *really wild leaders* seek to be fully in tune with their environment. It can change at any time, as can any situation or circumstance within it. They use each of their senses to determine exactly what is going on. This involves listening and observing well and picking up on even the most nuanced of signs, then deciding to communicate and act accordingly i.e., by choosing the right means for the right audience at the right time, in the right tone – demonstrating clarity, empathy (understanding) and encouragement.

The competitive world in which we operate can be dangerous and gruelling at times. Leaders will need to navigate their teams and stakeholders through some pretty tough times. By carefully choosing their words and demonstrating best actions, they will be far more likely to succeed.

How do you communicate with the range of your stakeholders? What do people hear you say? What do they see you doing? And what are the consequences?

## 6. Personally, connect and engage

*Really wild leaders* do not sit in their ivory towers. They lead from the front or work side by side in close proximity to their teams. Whilst modern leaders develop and use good reporting systems to provide the necessary insights to performance (of their teams, schools, government departments, companies or competitors for example), they also understand that without personally connecting and engaging with their stakeholders and the wider environment too, they will lose incredibly valuable context.

This will impact the quality and timeliness of their decisions and the opportunity to inspire and motivate their teams. Ultimately this will also impact the degree to which people will choose to follow and support them in their objectives.

The most wonderful examples of engagement are seen in schools where busy head teachers fully engage in the activities of their schools, when they take time to greet pupils and parents, to take a turn on playground duty and to make time to teach alongside their staff. I have observed that these leaders run happy schools, meet the needs of their very disparate cohorts who then go on to achieve in the most amazing ways. I have seen the opposite too where the life of the leader is filled only by spreadsheets, analyses and directives. Here, staff turnover, customer satisfaction and results will rarely compare.

I frequently meet strong business leaders too, who have enjoyed the most incredible support of their staff who have gone far beyond what is required of their roles or their official working hours. They have sought to get something done, not because they had to but because they wanted to. This would not have happened without a close connection and engagement by their leader.

Do you take time to personally connect and engage? If not, what can you change so you can?

## 7. Love people and the world about you

*"If your business genuinely improves people's lives success will follow." Richard Branso*n

People instinctively know whether someone actually cares for them. When they know their leader cares, they will often reciprocate with the most wonderful commitment and loyalty! This applies equally to staff, suppliers, partners, customers, pupils, parents and shareholders too.

It is by no mistake that the most senior executives who lead the happiest and most loyal of teams, show a genuine love for their people and the world. They appreciate the need to achieve short term targets to survive, but also value creating a long-term, healthy, happy and sustainable environment and results with which to thrive.

A *really wild leader* will take the time to notice the apparently little things knowing they could sometimes have a huge impact on the people or world around them. They then find ways to make a difference.

This could be by looking after a particular individual. It could be on a grander scale as they seek to develop a giving or environmental strategy way beyond the minimum requirements considered acceptable for corporate and social responsibility (CSR) purposes. It could also be putting standards and systems in place to safeguard and encourage the physical and mental wellbeing of staff and their families.

Whilst on a desert island a few years ago, my business partner noticed that a member of his team looked a little pale and clammy. He chose to enquire after her wellbeing rather than continue about his tasks for the day and realised very quickly that she had cut herself two days earlier and not told anyone about it. Had her injury gone unchecked for just another 24 hours she would have likely died from sepsis.

He was able to intervene and save her life.

As a leader, what are you doing to demonstrate love for the people and world around you? Are you paying sufficient attention? What effect do you have directly or indirectly on peoples' lives, their state of mental and physical wellbeing? Consider the environment you are creating and the natural world about you too!

### 8. Serve and remain humble

*Really wild leaders* encourage their teams to continually look out for one another, to find and act on opportunities to help. They do this most effectively by being seen to serve others themselves.

I was delighted to see this in action during an open day at a prestigious grammar school in the south east of England. Whilst hosting an important day for parents and teachers, the head master took time to clean up the mess from an over filled and knocked-over bin himself rather than instructing his students to do it. In this way they saw that he was serving them and that even he, in the most senior of positions, was not above doing even the most menial of tasks. Now isn't that somebody you would be happy to follow?

A leader's job is to set the direction and serve their team by creating the environment and securing the resources necessary for them to succeed.

What acts of service do you fulfill on a daily basis, to individuals close to you and for the organisation and extended community as a whole?

### 9. Be resilient

When making key decisions, the role of a leader can be a lonely one. Most decisions will be received differently by different audiences with criticism or attack sometimes coming more fervently than those of agreement or praise.

We have seen that a leader's values and principles may also sometimes be tested, and we instinctively know the physical, mental and personal strains one can face.

Resilience comes from looking after yourself, remaining authentic and by building and staying connected to the right support team of confidantes, loved ones and advisors around you. They care about you, believe in you and are confident enough to challenge you.

*Really wild leaders* are honest with themselves and take care of their physical and mental health.

They recognise their weaknesses as well as their strengths. They are not afraid to recognise when things are not going well or when they are ill, anxious or tired.

They are trained to share this information with their support group whenever such situations arise, and to then act upon the advice they are given. Failure to do so would be a disservice to themselves and neglection of their duty of care to others. You can't have a mountain leader ignore their possible exposure to altitude sickness, nor an Arctic leader a frost-bitten foot. The results would be disastrous. The same principles apply to leaders in commerce and public service.

What team do you have in place to support you in times of need? Who can help you with the difficult choices you make? What can you do to improve your own physical and mental health?

## 10. Be consistent but willing to change

People feel secure when their leaders are consistent in their behaviours.

A *really wild leader* is consistent in their actions but flexible in the path they choose to take, for the path they choose to take must change based upon results and changes in the environment around them.

It is my belief that wherever a leader chooses to lead their organisation, they can rest assured that if they are consistent in their application and development of the traits above, their chances of success will be high.

## Closing thoughts

Life is a great adventure and the adventure of leadership is indeed a rewarding one. For a *really wild leader*, it is incredible!

How do you measure up on the ten points above and where could you improve?

## References

- George B. (2008). *Discover your True North*. John Wiley & Sons.

## About Steven Shove

Steven is an experienced business leader, leadership and sales performance coach, a respected thought leader and one of the UK's most highly qualified survival instructors who passionately applies the principles of *original human success* to businesses, teams and individuals seeking to thrive in today's ever demanding and increasingly competitive environments.

For nearly 30 years, Steven consulted to and successfully led a variety of international teams and businesses, improving performance across the myriad of business functions and industries but specialising in leadership, sales, business strategy and personal development.

Steven is CEO and Founding Director of the *Really Wild Group* that offers performance improvement coaching and consulting services, educational events, executive retreats and expeditions to the business, education and leisure sectors.

Under his leadership, the team deploys a powerful and proven methodology for success that uniquely equips and enables all business functions and staff at every level, and students to deliver superior performance with far greater consistency and predictability - in the most exciting, engaging and memorable of ways.

Today, Steven works with clients in the boardroom or classroom and on leadership development retreats to remote places such as the wilds of the Arctic, the jungles of Borneo and our beautiful British and European woodlands.

www.reallywildbusiness.com

www.reallywildeducation.com

LinkedIn: linkedin.com/in/stevenshove

Facebook: Steven Shove https://www.facebook.com/steven.shove

Facebook: Really Wild Education https://www.facebook.com/ReallyWildED/

# Working On The Wrong Problem, Is The Problem

## Andrew Priestley

Problems are normal so it would be naive to think that life should have no problems. The issue is not problems, but how we react to and handle them. Especially as leaders.

There is a belief that the more successful you become the less problems you will get. This is not the case. The reality is, the more successful you become, the more problems you get to solve. But you get a different level of problems.

I tend to attract clients with complex operational or strategic problems. Knowledge and experience enables them to make the right decision and solve most problems quickly, most of the time.

I often coach team leaders working in high-end compliance, life and limb environments where problems typically need to be solved under pressure. In these environments, on a good day, if you fail to solve a problem or make a mistake you get fined heavily; and on a bad day someone gets injured or dies and you find yourself in front of a tribunal or even facing a criminal negligence lawsuit.

Over time, I developed a robust eight-step format to help my coaching clients unpack and resolve complex problems.

I recently coached a new team leader on a mining site.

The unofficial culture was to initiate new team members by having them detonate an explosive device with a very short fuse. This practice had its origins in the dim past when miners actually had to light short fuses. Today explosives are detonated remotely, from a safe distance, via radio control.

My client knew that this initiation is dangerous and illegal. It's all well and good if nothing bad happens, but the risk of injury was, historically, a distinct possibility.

Obviously, he could not ignore that risk, in a job already risky enough, but wanted to talk it through.

So here's how we unpacked that issue.

## 1. Describe The Situation

Start by describing what happened (or what's happening.) Just the basic story.

Importantly, unpack the sequence of events. What happened first, next, after that. Identify who was involved. Who were the key players, noting any key relationships or chain-of-command issues.

In this case, a long-standing leading hand was intent on upholding a rite-of-passage tradition. His firm belief was: This is what we've always done.

My client heard about this practice and immediately felt that this was not appropriate.

## 2. Identify The Real Problem

Next, rake over the situational elements carefully and explore: *Why is that a problem? What are the key concerns? Who would agree with me?*

You might also explore problem ownership: *who is this a problem for, exactly? Is this my problem, your problem; or ours?*

What you are attempting to do is identify the key problems; importantly, the *real* problem. Too often people get drawn into reacting to a situation rather than focusing on the *real* problem.

He was well-aware of the obvious issues: safety, illegality, litigation. And he was certain that if anything went wrong and there was an inquiry, and it could be demonstrated that he knew about the stunt and let it proceed, he would, technically, be liable.

But my client was sheepish.

He was worried about being accepted as a new team leader. He was concerned that he would end up being ostracised for interfering with a work site tradition by enforcing a safety requirement. He was worried that he would then lose the cooperation of his team.

Exploring a situation to discover *why* something is a problem usually uncovers the real problem. In this case, the real problem was putting his own needs to be accepted ahead of safety.

### 3. Explore The Implications of Doing Nothing

Step 2 often identifies the solution but it's important to resist the urge to implement any solution just yet.

Explore questions like: *What happens if I do nothing? If this continues? What are the explicit and implicit implications, risks, consequences?*

My client was very quick to remind me that if this initiation backfired there would be an inquiry where the company could be penalised, fined or sued for criminal negligence. And, he could be sued for personal negligence and lapse of duty-of-care, also. The leading hand had certainly *initiated* many of the workers without consequence but this initiation certainly had a foreseeable element of risk that my client was understandably concerned about. Especially, if he did nothing.

Why is *doing nothing* a problem? In this case, it sends the message that the unwanted behaviour is acceptable or will be tolerated. And that becomes part of the safety culture: it's OK to ignore safety.

One option that shaped his decision to bar this practice was imaging the initiation going wrong and having to explain to his employer and a barrister in an inquiry why he allowed this to proceed.

## 4. Explore The Benefits of Doing Something

Next, explore the explicit positive benefits of doing something proactive or constructive. *What are the benefits?* And: *who benefits?*

In this case, most of the workers were men with young families. He felt that he would never be able to explain to a family why their loved one had been injured or killed performing a prank.

The obvious key benefit is safe work site. Mining sites are dangerous enough without adding additional risks.

Stopping this behaviour sends a clear message about safety and studies show, contributes to a safe work site culture.

## 5. Consider Your Options

The key task here is to slow down and consider your options. Flush out your best thinking. Explore whether remedial, adaptive or full proactive options are required?

Often, people skip this step. We naturally don't like problems so we tend to knee-jerk a solution - usually the wrong one - when we fail to consider a broader range of options.

In reality there are three key options: *do nothing, do something indirect* or *do something direct.*

The *do nothing* option basically means do nothing. Don't intervene. One *do something indirect* option might be to ask a subordinate to deal with the situation. The *do something direct* option is to talk directly to the leading hand, then call a team meeting and address the issue head-on. Each option deserves exploration.

## 6. Select A Solution

This step requires you to decide which solution to implement, ensuring that it is appropriate and resourceful. And legal.

My client spoke to his leading hand, who agreed to drop the practice. He then called a meeting of the team and informed them that it was no longer acceptable to initiate workers by handling live explosives.

He said that worker and site safety was paramount and that he was required to uphold *Health and Safety* requirements and laws. He acknowledged that while this was a long standing work site, rite-of-passage it was no longer a practice he would condone or tolerate.

## 7. Implementation/Monitoring/Feedback

At this stage, explore how you will implement the solution; and determine how you will know it is working. Or not.

Essentially, the problem is a non-stakeholder of the company was implementing a dangerous practice and expected his employer to look the other way. This is technically insubordination.

The meeting was cordial and short. He opened the floor for discussion and there was none. However, very quickly, he was having private asides with various staff who felt the leading hand was essentially shaming, goading or intimidating new staff into performing this stunt. No one considered this ritual fun or appropriate.

## 8. Review/Repeat/Exit

This step is about assessing whether the solution has reached the intended conclusion.

Regrettably, the leading hand implemented a clandestine initiation which resulted in the leading hand being suspended, and then dismissed. The team were again debriefed and safety training was implemented and scheduled quarterly.

It is important to note that this format doesn't just apply to high-risk scenarios. It can apply to most problem solving situations that you will encounter, where there is inferred complexity or the pressure to resolve an issue quickly.

No one likes problems. Subsequently, people typically jump from the *Situation* (Step 1) to a *Solution* (Step 6). Invariably, if a problem isn't resolving easily, or at all, then most likely you have skipped or rushed important steps. And you will be working on the wrong problem.

In my experience, Steps 2 and 3 provide immense clarity to a leader because a) you uncover the *real* problem; and b) by considering the implications of *doing nothing,* intensify the need for an effective resolution.

As a result, the benefits are amplified, especially when we are talking about problems with a high opportunity cost. And you tend to identify more appropriate options.

Importantly, this process is designed to slow the game right down. I have countless examples of clients who successfully applied this format with great effect, simply because they took time to unpack the problem.

This process invariably identifies complexities and flushes out the *real* problem. In my experience, working on the wrong problem … is the problem.

## About Andrew Priestley

Andrew Priestley is a qualified, award winning business coach, speaker and best-selling author.

He is head coach for *Dent Global,* ranked in the *Top 100 Entrepreneur Mentors* in the UK; and is the founder of *LeadershipGigs,* a global business leadership think tank.

He works with established SMEs and larger clients, worldwide.

Andrew is the Chairman of the Trustees for the *Clear Sky Childrens' Charity,* UK and provides NED services for select clients.

www.andrewpriestley.com

https://www.linkedin.com/in/andrew-priestley-tce/

## Emerging Trends

**Innovation, disruption, new thinking,
gaps in the market, emerging industries,
emerging trends, transitions, transformations**

# Technology, the Promise, Prize, Problem And Proposal For Thriving In Business In The Digital Era

## Natalie Jameson

Technology and innovation are outpacing regulation and labour skills. We are also living and leading through several simultaneous political and demographic giga-trends. These trends are crashing into each other to shift governmental powers, wealth as well as blurring the lines of competition. The trends present opportunities with little or no barriers to entry to disruptive innovators. Globally connected *giggers* are taking big bites of the lunches of established incumbents across all markets. Like it or not every enterprise needs to think digital first.

### Promise and Prize

Robots, machines and artificial intelligence hold the beautiful promise that humanity can be free to get on with applying our touchy-feely, emotional, moral and intellectual abilities. Essentially what is humane.

Digitalisation can unchain us from the mundane, to dream up solutions for a sustainable existence on our planet. Imagine if we all knew how to conceptualise the use tech to achieve a kinder more equally distributed system of healthcare, wealth and power, despite the volatile and complex circumstances in which we live? Imagine if you harnessed the power of tech for a more profitable, purposeful business? Think about how delighted your staff and customers would be if you used data and insights to listen and respond to their needs. How much would customers be willing to pay if you were able to predict their needs and deliver a solution at or before the point of pain? Wow right?

These things are all possible with technology.

As are missions, to change the world or agitate a traditional industry, that can be started in the back bedroom of any man, woman or even child regardless of race, age, economic, health or physical abilities.

Technology provides a pathway for everyone and every organisation to live and work delivering profits and impact in flexible ways, in a portfolio of side businesses and personal purpose projects.

The trend for side business is on the rise an estimated that 30% of UK workers have one and many more are intending to do the same. Basically tech is magic. Right? Well there is a catch.

To collect on this technological promise and prize we are reliant on the equal participation in and collective application of digital technologies of all people. We must especially have our children and workforce being able to communicate, contribute and comprehend digital technology uses, language and skills.

## Problem

So are we all in the game? Well not so much. We are facing a digital skills crisis with an estimated 12.6 million[1] adults lacking the basic digital skills needed to cope in our modern society, and 5.8 million adults have never used the internet at all.

The UK has a *hella-huge* digital literacy deficit which according to Parliament is costing the economy an eye-watering £63 billion a year in lost additional GDP.

Oh, and then there is robo the cobot that is interviewing for your job as we speak. The *World Economic Forum* estimates that 1.4m roles will be displaced or made redundant by new technologies in eight years. 57% of those job will be women's.

So far this call to all has yet to translate into wide scale retraining of our workforce. However I don't think we should feel threatened that we can't compete with the scale, speed and accuracy that a  machine can perform calculation, repetition, statistical analysis and predictive tasks.

Actually, good, these things are dull and machines can't do what is innately humane.  Therefore by retraining  we will be absolutely fine.  A machine can learn to read expression and categorise emotions but they can't solve problems with empathy, ethics, creativity and relationships which are all humanly gratifying. So bring it on, bots!

Bots  aside, at the risk of sounding over dramatic, unless we address the skills gaps we will turn our current parity issues into irreversible chasm of social and economic inequality. Yeah that was OTT. But I actually believe it.

As a business community we will be opening up a global can of competitive kick-butt and be staring down the barrel of major productivity problems if we don't retrain our people. Not to mention once we get behind as a nation in the innovation stakes – we won't really have much  going for us as we aren't the manufacturing nation we once were.

If at this point if I have made you feel like you want to lay down in the road and be run over by an autonomous car, read on. I will share what I have seen work in the real world  which you can put into play to harness the promise and prize of digital, as a leader, if you haven't already.

## The Proposal

Become a vivid visionary leader with a purpose-aligned, learning and innovative organisation.

PURPOSE LED BUSINESS BULB
GET A VIVID VISION & TURN THE LIGHT
ON INNOVATION

**CORE PURPOSE & INTEGRATED IMPACT**
The business is an expression of purpose and what our stakeholders believe in. Only people who care deeply about our purpose are on the mission with us. We have integrated impact through organisations like B1G1 and alignment with UN Sustainable Development Goals

**COLLECTIVELY CAPABLE CODIFIED CURIOSITY**
We own or can access the vital capability through collaboration. Curiosity and learning are cultural Missteps are vital to our evolved capability. We ask what's now - what's next, what's next next of ourselves & everyone we meet everyday.

**WORLD IS CALLING OUT**
We don't make things for the sake of it wasting the planet's resources. We are addressing an real unmet We keep innovating to answer the current call for action

**COMMERCIALLY VIABLE**
The world is willing & able to pay for it or devote resources for it.

- **Attract Talent With Ethical Profit To Purpose-Realignment.**
  Become a force for good and step into purposeful authentic leadership by joining a growing tribe that is *mothering earth* and her citizens.

  Purpose drives people and people drive performance.

  Today's talent and loyal customers want to get behind a brand they can voluntarily advocate and social proof on it's behalf.

  There is a genuine expectation that business should take the lead to drive social and environmental change where government regulation is absent or inadequate.

- **Plug & Pivot.** Innovate new business models and curate value creation. Savvy companies can pilot new ideas, pivot markets and products with relative ease by plugging into others' entrepreneurial ability. Joint ventures and collective bundling can bring new value to your customers or new customer group. Typically these can be hub and spoke in nature to make them pacey and agile. These will only work if curated by future-fit leaders and supplemented by talent (which by the way you will only attract if your business presents a promising opportunity to get behind a cause, movement or something cutting edge).

- **Innovate At The Front Line.** Innovation happens at the front line not just in the boardroom. You and your front line staff must have a wide-angle view of yours and your customers' world and be looking it through a digital lens. If your whole organisation isn't aware of the art of the possible, open their eyes. If they don't have a creative problem solving toolbox like a design thinking methodology get them one. This is crucial for eureka moments for potential new customer solutions.

- **Retrain To Retain Talent.** In most cases replacing employees only winds up costing more than upskilling. By the time you've lost the goodwill and investment made to date on that employee. Possibly valuable client relationships, then pile on the recruiting manager's time and finders fees it can cost tens of thousands to replace an employee earning £30k. But if that were the only issue, you may consider it for the long-term return on investment. The digital skills gap is a nation/world-wide phenomenon. The talent *isn't* out there as proven by the millions of unfilled digital-age positions.

Basically, the future isn't a destination that you get in shape for, then relax. Like anything diet, fitness, writing, being future-fit as an organisation needs new habits. By building in curiosity, learning, mini experiments, trying out one-project stands with various partners you will start to be the type of agile organisation that talent wants to work for and customers want to buy from. Where curiosity and collaboration deepens relationships and advocacy extends the life time value of your customers as well as reaching whole new audiences.

You and your workforce can build the habits to problem solve with a digital mindset and kick butt in rapid in G-force conditions of unpredictable, perpetual, radical, continuous and accelerating change. Good luck!

### Think digital - leadership reflection points and habits

- Are we capable either on our own or collectively through collaboration?

- Is curiosity codified and is learning cultural?

- Are we diverse in our thinking and capability as an organisation and could we add diversity and creativity through NED, hiring or partnerships?

- Are we recording missteps as opportunities to learn regularly in our team meetings?

- Do we know our peoples current future-of-work skills capability - such as relational, communication, empathy, emotional intelligence or creativity?

- Do we have a *moon-shot* mindset i.e., do our staff know the art of the possible? If not could we have regular workshops or invite innovative start-ups , developers or thought-leaders to share the world of tech and how it is shaping our world and our customer's?

- Do we ask: *What's now? What's next?, What's next-next?,* of ourselves and everyone we meet everyday?

- Are we making something that the world is still calling out for? How do we know that to be fact?

- Do we know who else solves problems for our customers and could we bring this in-house with technology?

- Could we innovate ways to create value for our clients whilst creating a smaller imprint?

- When was that last time we developed anything new in response to a customer or business pain point?

- Do we set innovation as a budgetary challenge for our people to create new revenue streams ?

- Do we make things for the sake of profit alone wasting the planet's resources?

- Is our business an expression of purpose and what our stakeholders believe in?

- Are people who care deeply about our purpose on the mission with us?

- Have we have integrated impact through organisations like *B1G1 www.b1g1.com/businessforgood/* or alignment with *UN Sustainable Development Goals?*

- Are the things we make high impact, low imprint on the earth's resources, high return with the right risk mix?

## Reference

- [1] https://www.bbc.co.uk/news/business-36510266

## About Natalie Jameson

Natalie is CEO at *Heroworx Innovation & Startup Labs.*

Natalie and her team equip founders to harness their Innovation DNA to start, buy or build a futureproof, financially secure digital business whilst making an impact in the world. Her approach to business comes from the learnings from a 25 year portfolio career lending 100's of millions for midmarket B2B acquisitions, Co-founding the UK's first eight figure, six site, dental company in *Sainsburys* and *Tesco* sold to *BUPA* '13, commercial architectural redesign gigs, business strategy consulting, digital transformation for *food and bev.* She holds a BA in Interior Architectural Design and Postgrad in Business and Finance.

Natalie mentors Manchester tech-startups, advocates for diversity in tech and on boards, is co-developing a tech-based one-page social impact business plan, authoring a white paper on the future of women at work. She's always seeking targets, collaborations and talent to execute her buy and build ambitions for *Heroworx.*

Natalie's a California can *do-ist* who seeks magic at the intersection of humanity and technology, loves family, learning, mentoring, art, Manchester, hot yoga, wine and girls weekends and *B1G1.com.*

Facebook https://www.facebook.com/heroworx.io

Twitter https://twitter.com/njco2design

LinkedIn www.linkedin.com/in/natheroworx

Website Http://heroworx.io

Instagram https://www.instagram.com/natheroworx/

# Did You Miss
# Fit-For-Purpose Leadership #1, #2 or #3?

The best-selling *Fit-For-Purpose Leadership* #1, #2 and 3 are all available on *Amazon* as both paperback and *Kindle*. In each edition, inspired leaders worldwide share their highest-value, current best thinking on business leadership.

Watch out for *Fit-For-Purpose Leadership #5*, coming soon!

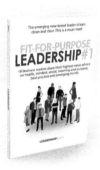

# Join Leadership Gigs

Would you like to be a part of *Leadership Gigs*? *Leadership Gigs* is a confidential forum for business leaders worldwide.

It operates as a closed *Whatsapp* and *Facebook* community. Our aim for this is to build a thriving community of business leaders who are helping each other's journey into the next decade.

One of the benefits is the opportunity to share your highest value thinking in the bestselling *Fit For Purpose Leadership* book series, published twice a year.

A good way to start to get involved is by requesting to join our *Facebook* group:

*http://bit.ly/LeadershipGigsFB*